DERAILED
ON THE
BIPOLAR EXPRESS

By Joie Edson

Martin Sisters Publishing

Published by
Martin Sisters Publishing Company, Inc.
www. martinsisterspublishing. com
Copyright © 2018 Joie Edson

ISBN: 978-1-62553-990-8

Memoir
Edited by Renee Belcastro
Printed in the United States of America

For Tommy

DEDICATION

This book is dedicated to the parents and families raising children who are coping with mood disorders. We shall travel on this journey together, and by sharing our stories, someday minimize the stigma associated with mental illness.

ACKNOWLEGEMENTS

I wish to thank everyone who has coaxed, coached, convinced, and even threatened me to *finally* share my story of raising two sons with mental illness.

Foremost, I want to thank Jim for his scrupulous editing skills and unwavering support. More than two years ago, I shared with him my goal to write this book. I told him that I didn't know how to begin the book, I couldn't remember the chronological order of all the events. The details of the past 15 years were easy to recall, but the timeline was foggy. He suggested that I begin anywhere. Precise dates weren't important. Sharing my story was what mattered the most. He patiently offered his assistance with the editing along the way, but most importantly, provided me with compassion and love as I poured out my soul on each page.

Kisses and hugs to my dear friend June, who offered to read and review my story as I wrote each chapter. The wisdom, advice, and wit she provided helped me to stay on track and keep on writing.

Thank you to my daughter, JoEllen. Her constant, yet not so gentle, reminder that I promised her father that I would someday chronicle our family's journey gave me the impetus to finally begin writing. Many times, she urged me to "write the damn book" and often threatened to beat me to it.

I also would like to thank the Massachusetts Department of Mental Health, the Wakefield Police Department, and the countless psychiatrists, therapists, and social workers throughout Massachusetts who have aided my sons.

Most of all, I want to thank TJ and Kayvon. Thank you both for allowing me to frankly and openly share your story. I love you and hope you continue to grow in strength, wisdom, and acceptance.

CHAPTERS

CHAPTER ONE

Fasten Your Seatbelts.

It's Going to Be a Bumpy Ride

He was in front of me, bent over with his shorts pulled down below his knees, taunting me. "You want your car key? It's in there. Come and get it." I was appalled and disgusted. He had taken my car key and shoved it up his ass. Although this was not the most profound or notable act that my son had committed against me, it was one of the most disturbing.

I awoke to the sound of my doorbell early that morning. My initial thought was that I wasn't expecting a package to be delivered that early in the day. Then a familiar sense of dread took over. My heart began to race at the realization that my son was paying me an unexpected visit at 7:00 a.m. Early morning visits meant trouble. He was unable to sleep due to mania. He would be demanding money. His behavior would be erratic and unpredictable. I hesitated, taking a deep breath, before opening the door.

The visit, as typical, began pleasantly enough. He looked disheveled with dark circles and hooded eyes from lack of sleep. I was wary, yet I welcomed him in and offered him breakfast. He told me he just needed to use my dryer to dry his clothes. He had gotten soaked in the rain from driving his scooter the 10-mile trip from his Boston apartment to my condo. We exchanged a few pleasantries. His mood was labile: one minute calm, the next sad, then angry. While petting our family dog, he started to cry, expressing his sadness that she was getting old and would not be with us much longer. Soon, the demands began. "I'm broke. You need to give me my money. It's my money, not yours. You are my Representative Payee and you are, by law, supposed to give me my money when I need it." I informed him that his monthly payment for Social Security Disability had run out. I offered to give him $20 to hold him over. "That's not enough. I need at least $150." I refused. That refusal set him off.

He took my phone and demanded that I transfer money into his account. I told him I wanted him to leave immediately. I felt threatened and began screaming at him to give me back my phone or I would call the police. He confiscated my iPad next, once again demanding a transfer of funds. I begged him to give me back my phone and iPad and threatened to drive to the police station if he didn't leave my condo. That's when he grabbed my keys, removed my car key from the chain, and shoved it up his ass. I became hysterical and began chasing him around my condo, pleading with him to return my car key. At one point a physical fight ensued and he threatened me with a knife. I left my condo and ran to the police station, which thankfully was only one-half mile away.

When I arrived at the police station, I was met by an officer familiar with me and my family. Unfortunately, for better or worse, the entire town is familiar with me and my family. There have been countless calls and trips to the police station over the past 15 years. The female officer sensed the reason for my visit as soon as I walked in looking desperate and ashamed. She invited me to take a seat. "Looks like you're having a bad day. Trouble again? Don't worry … things will eventually get better." I turned to her and asked, "Will things ever get better? I'm not so sure about that."

While telling my best friend about this most recent, disturbing incident, she turned to me and stated, "It's another chapter for your book." Countless times I've been told I need to write a book about the trials and tribulations of raising two boys who suffer from bipolar disorder 1 with psychosis. Their father, prior to his death from terminal stage 4 cancer, requested, as a dying wish, that I write a book. I have tried, on several occasions, during the past 15 years to begin writing. What has prolonged this process is the fact that I don't remember every hospitalization, every arrest, or every conviction that has led to the time my sons have spent in jail due to the severity of their mental illness. The dates and the details of every psychotic and manic episode have become blurred in the past 15 years.

I've even questioned the purpose of writing the book. Will anyone want to read about the life of an ordinary woman who has unfortunately had to learn to survive extraordinary events caused by the psychotic episodes of her two mentally ill sons? Perhaps you are reading this book to gain insight on coping with a family member who has mental illness. Perhaps you just want to read about the bizarre and dysfunctional behavior caused by people who suffer from bipolar disorder. Maybe you simply want advice from someone who has learned to cope.

I hope you are not reading this book to judge my sons or myself. Raising children who suffer from mental illness is a lifelong struggle. It is a journey with many twists and turns. I have made many mistakes and taken countless wrong turns along the way. During the past 15 years, I have learned more about negotiating the mental health system, the criminal justice system, and the correctional system than I ever wanted to. I have been a staunch and relentless advocate for my sons.

What I'm hoping you'll gain from reading this book is hope. This is a story of survival, acceptance, and redemption. This story is not simply about me. It is about my family and our journey.

CHAPTER TWO

Backpack on the Boston Marathon Finish Line

Many times, when asked how I deal with having to raise two sons who suffer from mental illness, my stock response has always been, "Things could be worse." I've never wanted a pity party. I hear about parents who must care for children with chronic life-threatening physical illnesses or children who die suddenly from a tragic death. My heart goes out to anyone who has a physically ill child, whether the illness is chronic or acute. I wonder how this misery would be different from the struggle I will always deal with.

Quite frankly, I think the most prominent difference is that raising a child with mental illness can be humiliating. I am embarrassed to admit that I have often been ashamed and humiliated by very public displays of psychosis caused by my sons. A parent who has a child suffering from a physical chronic illness such as cancer is surrounded by sympathy and support. A parent who has a child like mine is often blamed for or accused by others of the events caused from their child's illness. The visible symptoms of physical illness, such as baldness or deformity, evoke reactions quite different from the symptoms caused by mental illness. Mania, psychosis,

11

depression, suicidal thoughts, and delusions are invisible. It's difficult to empathize with someone else's emotions because they can't be seen. The community doesn't rally together to hold fundraisers, road races, walkathons, or send care baskets to a child who is diagnosed with mental illness. It's a lonely and often humbling illness to bear. Honestly, it sucks a lot.

The bombing that occurred on April 15, 2013, at the Boston Marathon finish line will forever be etched in the memories of Bostonians and the world. However, one year later, an event occurred, at that same location that also became local, national, and international news. And it involved my son.

My husband Tom, our daughter, and I were attending a town meeting in Newbury, Massachusetts on April 15, 2014. Tom and I owned a beach house and needed to gain permission from the conservation commission to make improvements on our property. My daughter, JoEllen, an oncology nurse, accompanied us to the meeting because we needed her medical assistance and emotional support. The timing of the meeting was inconvenient, yet necessary. Tom was in the end stages of stage 4 head and neck cancer. He had been diagnosed with Stage 4 squamous cell carcinoma 11 months prior to the meeting and had undergone intense chemotherapy and radiation. The cancer was still growing and had spread to his lungs requiring a tracheotomy. Tom had a difficult time speaking, so JoEllen and I were presenting our case in front of the conservation commission. We had silenced our phones during the lengthy two-hour meeting.

It was a dark and rainy drive home. We were mentally exhausted, and Tom was uncomfortable from sitting on a hard bench during the lengthy meeting. I recall having a difficult time navigating the back roads to the highway while driving due to the heavy downpours and flooded roads. Once I had safely reached the highway, JoEllen realized we had not yet turned on our phones. She was in the backseat of my car when I heard her fiddling with her cellphone. I still recall her voice shaking as she gasped and then exclaimed, "Oh, no ... God, no ... Mom, we need to pull over." I asked why I needed to stop driving, immediately thinking that someone we knew was injured or worse, had died. She began sobbing and pleaded that I pull over. Tom began gesturing, by vigorously pointing to the highway, for us to keep driving. He just wanted to get home to rest. He was exhausted and in dire need of pain medication. I refused to pull over and insisted that JoEllen tell us what was happening. By now, she was sobbing hysterically. "Everyone is trying to reach us. I have about 10 messages. Kayvon has put a backpack on the Boston Marathon finish line." The panic I immediately felt was palatable.

I don't know how we made it home. JoEllen began frantically reciting every message as I drove. "It's all over the news, on every news station...He's been arrested...They think he had a bomb." I was appalled, incredulous, and heartbroken. How could he do this? What was he thinking? What kind of a monster is he? My own son. I recall saying that he should rot in hell. I can still feel the hatred I had for him at that time. My own son. Tom was nearly catatonic, staring at the road ahead speechless. For the remainder of the ride home he simply stared silently at the road ahead. When we pulled into our driveway, only three hours after our son left that notorious backpack on the marathon finish line, it was as if all hell broke loose.

While driving down the street, to our typically quiet neighborhood located in the suburbs of Boston, we saw news vans equipped with tall antennas and bright lights surrounding the area in front of our home. We drove up our long driveway and ran into the house. JoEllen was on her cellphone, and friends were strongly suggesting that we pull down our shades, keep our house dark, and shut off our home phone. When I picked up my home phone I already had at least a dozen phone calls from national news stations such as CBS, NBC, and Fox TV requesting interviews. I had messages from Diane Sawyer of ABC and *Inside Edition*. How did they know who I was, discover where I lived and find out my home telephone number? Social media, as anyone knows, is a blessing and a curse. In this case, our Facebook accounts led the media to us, along with many unknown and ignorant people who posted nasty and hurtful comments in our news feeds. We shut down our Facebook accounts, but most of the damage already had been done. There is no such thing as privacy once news goes viral on social media. My doorbell rang, and a Wakefield Police officer rescued us once again. I want to interject here. Over the many years of physical altercations, arrests, and countless hospitalizations that have occurred due to my son's struggles with mental illness, the Wakefield Police have been a source of comfort, professionalism, and strength. They have never judged me or my family. They have treated us all, including my sons, with dignity. The officers of the Wakefield Police Department are well trained in handling emergent psychiatric situations. Kudos to them! The officer who rang our doorbell, entered our home and told us to feel free to call them if anyone tried to enter our property. He informed us that the media and the press were not allowed on our property. He also told us that they would send cruisers to keep the neighborhood safe while the media was parked in front of our house. The circus had come to town and invaded our neighborhood, yet we were the unintentional ringleaders.

One phone message that I had received while driving home was of upmost importance. A Boston police officer contacted us, informing us where Kayvon was being held for questioning and mental health evaluation. He asked that we contact him. All the hatred and despise I had held toward my son earlier in the evening began to dissolve as I listened to his recount of the situation. Kayvon was extremely manic and now, locked in a cell being questioned about terrorism and bombs, was rapidly beginning to mentally unravel. He told us the police, positioned at the Boston Marathon finish line, became overly cautious. They had received calls that a suspicious character, dressed in black clothing and a black veil, was marching near the finish line chanting "Boston Strong." They surrounded Kayvon and insisted that he take off his backpack and inquired of the contents. All the while, news cameras were actively documenting the scene. Even though Kayvon assured them he only had a rice cooker filled with his business cards, they took the backpack, placed it on the finish line and detonated it. This is what the entire world initially witnessed on television, in newspapers, and the internet.

To this day, Kayvon will tell you that this was all an elaborate performance. At the time, in his mania-driven mind, he thought that it was a good idea to initiate this "symbolic form of performance art" on the one-year anniversary of the Boston Marathon bombings. Mania causes the mentally ill person to feel invincible, grandiose, impulsive, and promiscuous. Common sense no longer applies. At the time, Kayvon was a student, attending the Massachusetts College of Art. His major, Studio of Integrated Media, encouraged "thinking outside the box." Kayvon, a particularly talented student, fueled by mania, initiated this performance believing it was to be viewed as incredibly moving work of art. He never mentioned his intentions to his family or any of his fellow students, friends, or the professors at Mass Art. Had he done that, I'm certain they would've told him his timing was far less than ideal.

I can still see Kayvon's frightened face, with macabre make-up dripping down his face, filling television screens on every major network. He was terrified and confused. I was relieved to see that he already had a lawyer assigned to his case who was stressing, very publicly, that Kayvon had bipolar disorder and was not aware of the extent of his actions. His intentions were not criminal. He wasn't trying to hurt anyone. His lawyer, a public defender who willingly took his case pro bono, turned out to be a tremendous blessing. She possesses enormous empathy for the mentally ill as she, herself, has a mentally ill family member. Shannon O'Leary has since become a strong advocate for individuals who are arrested while manic, depressed, or psychotic. Court systems all over the world need more individuals like Ms. O'Leary.

Kayvon was transported to Bridgewater State Hospital for psychiatric evaluation the next day. He was held in that facility for nearly a month while he awaited trial. Classifying Bridgewater State Hospital as a psychiatric treatment facility is akin to calling McDonald's a fine dining establishment. Bridgewater State Hospital is a jail. Mentally ill inmates are held at the facility while awaiting trial, until they are deemed mentally capable of standing trial. They receive minimal psychiatric treatment, mostly in the form of psychiatric medications, and virtually no cognitive or behavioral therapy. Patients are housed in cells. The facility itself is surrounded by barbed electrical wire and watched by guards. This was not the first time either of my sons was committed to this facility. Sadly, it was not my first rodeo.

The remainder of the evening was spent speaking on our cellphones to friends and relatives who offered advice, support, and comfort. We assured them we would not open our Facebook pages and read the horrendous remarks made about Kayvon and our family. We convinced them we would keep our shades down, lights dim, not answer the phone or the door, and try to get some sleep. I was in survival mode. Did I have enough groceries to get through the next couple of days? Did Tom have enough medication? How was I going to let our dog out to do her business? When dealing with a situation like this, I've always resorted to compartmentalization. I couldn't handle Kayvon at the moment, so I did as much as possible to help make the situation manageable. I trudge through. I don't dwell. I survive.

The next morning, I spoke with Attorney O'Leary. She filled me in on the legalities of Kayvon's charges and assured me that he would not be held at Bridgewater State Hospital any longer than absolutely necessary. She also warned me about speaking to or contacting the press or media. I was torn. It was extremely enticing for me to finally have the opportunity to publicly discuss the woes of the mental health system. I finally had an opportunity and a captive audience. Kayvon's case would draw media attention to the shortfalls of mental health care. However, I held back, because she assured me that my comments may hurt his case in the long run.

I also have been extremely fortunate to have a strong support system of friends and family members who have stood by us during the worst of times. Friends and family came to our house, armed with food, to sit with us and offer comfort. They marched bravely by the media and dodged questions. When I felt that I just needed to step outside to get fresh air, they helped to conceal me. They read the statement I sent to *The Boston Globe* and rallied. My friends have always told me that I am the strongest person they know. They remark on my ability to stay positive in the most trying of times. I suppose I am strong, but what are the other choices? If I allow my sons' mental illnesses to wear me down, depress me, or make me cynical, the illness wins. I will not be defeated by their illnesses, symptoms, and resulting ramifications. I did not cause their illness, nor can I cure or control their illness. Most importantly, I can't let their illnesses ruin my life. I can rally for them, advocate for better care and assistance, offer support, and love them, but I need to take care of me. During the 15 years of sheer craziness, I have realized that taking care of me is what has made the difference. Whether it be going to the gym, having coffee or dinner with a good friend, or simply blocking calls from a son who is maniacally insisting I give him more money, I take my own little mental health vacations.

CHAPTER THREE
The Bail Out

Sometimes, when dealing with implications of mental illness, you must resort to extreme measures. Often, when looking back at this particular incident, I realize that desperation led to some extreme and actually very comical measures.

As promised, Kayvon was held at Bridgewater State Hospital for only two weeks. He was kept in protective custody due to the notoriety of his case. During those two weeks, national interest waned and the general public came to realize that he was just "another crazy person." Massachusetts College of Art, initially sending us a certified letter notifying us that Kayvon was suspended from their institution and no longer welcome near the campus, changed face and actually began supporting his freedom of expression. The faculty and students began to rally and support him. It must be noted here that a very high percentage of artists and art students are diagnosed with mental illness. His professors recognized that, despite his lack of common sense surrounding the timing of his elaborate performance, the freedom to express any type of art needs to be protected.

On the day of Kayvon's trial, the courtroom was nearly full of friends, fellow students, and faculty from Mass Art. I was moved and encouraged by this overwhelming demonstration of support. I attended court with JoEllen and my mother. The trial was highly publicized, and I was warned, by Ms. O'Leary, to stay away from the press. I had to keep my head down and run past the microphones that were forced in front of me. Little did anyone know that I was attending this trial armed with $50,000 cash. Specifically, $25,000 in each bra cup.

A few days before the trial, Ms. O'Leary notified me that Kayvon would possibly be let of jail if we came up with bail in the amount of $50,000. She inquired whether we were in the financial position to come up with such an enormous amount of money in a short amount of time. Luckily, we had taken out a home equity loan and were in the position to garner the bail. She assured us that we would eventually get the bail money back once the charges were dropped. Tom was not so sure and very wary about trusting that the charges would get dropped. I convinced him that we needed to do this in order to get Kayvon out of Bridgewater State Hospital while awaiting trial. He reluctantly agreed. I went to the bank, withdrew the funds in cash, and sewed $25,000 in each of my bra cups. Why? Because I was informed by Ms. O'Leary that the bail money needed to be paid in cash, and I wasn't going into Boston with $50,000 in my pocket!

I can still recall the incredulous look on the bailer's face when I signed the paperwork to bail Kayvon out and began taking $50,000 out of my bra. Little did we know that I could not produce that large of an amount of bail in cash. I needed a certified check and I needed it by the time court closed or Kayvon would be sent back to Bridgewater. I only had one hour!

JoEllen and I began our one-hour frantic trek to several banks within walking distance of the courthouse. Two banks refused our request for a certified check because we didn't have accounts in their institutions. We raced to a nearby Bank of America with only 20 minutes to spare. Because it was such a large amount of money, I had to fill out all sorts of lengthy paperwork before receiving the certified check in the amount of $50,000. Otherwise, I could be charged with money laundering. We only had 10 minutes to spare when we left the bank. We hopped in a taxi and arrived at the courthouse, certified check in hand, with two minutes to spare. We saved Kayvon from being transported back to Bridgewater State Hospital in the nick of time. He was fitted with an ankle electronic tracking device, told not to leave the state, and to check in with probation regularly. He was coming home.

Four years have passed since this event. I'm reflecting upon this event on Kayvon's 28th birthday, still trying to wrap my head around the fact that Kayvon still has no remorse surrounding the event, even though it deeply traumatized his family. He is still on probation and not yet able to travel outside of the country without permission. He was found "not guilty" on most counts but held responsible for creating a "public nuisance." His case was "Continued Without a Finding." His father, who passed from cancer less than two months after this event, adamantly felt that Kayvon should've been held accountable and served jail time. He died without the ability to ever forgive Kayvon.

The bail money was eventually returned in its entirety. My son, whom we named Kevin, never returned to me the same. He has become an anomaly. As talented as he is, he needed 10 years to complete his course work to graduate from The Massachusetts College of Art. He walked with his graduating class in 2016 but received an empty diploma. He completed his last two courses six months later. He now insists that we call him Kayvon. He is a nonconformist who often hurts his friends and family with biting and offensive, unforgivable remarks that he publicly posts on social media in order to draw attention to himself. When using social media as a form of blackmail, he sabotages relationships. The lines of right and wrong are totally blurred. He struggles to fit into the norms of society. Along with being diagnosed with bipolar disorder, he has since been diagnosed with an underlying personality disorder. I wonder if he'll ever be able to seek employment or live independently.

It's difficult to admit, I didn't celebrate his 28th birthday with him. I sent him a birthday card with a $200 gift card for food. No matter how much I give him, it's never enough. He's never thankful and his expectations are often absurd. Perhaps I should've simply ignored his birthday, but this is the struggle I often have when raising sons with mental illness.

Twenty-nine years ago, I gave birth to a 6-pound, 11-ounce son. As with all mothers of newborns, I fell in love instantly. I imagined who he'd grow up to be, the wonderful things he'd accomplish, and the love he'd spread. Nineteen years later, when he was first diagnosed with bipolar disorder, it all changed. Yet, with all the disappointment I have in my heart today, I hold on to the hope that things will someday be better. Because I am his mother and he is sick.

CHAPTER FOUR

Lady Gaga and Google

Mania often presents itself in a very comical and quite absurd manner. As JoEllen often says, "You just can't make this shit up!" Both Kayvon and TJ have experienced manic or psychotic episodes that at the time were frightening and serious yet are often quite comedic. And, as a mother of someone suffering from a manic episode, it certainly lessens the anxiety to simply laugh. Finding comedy in the midst of tragedy is a wonderful coping mechanism. Kayvon was fascinated and obsessed with Lady Gaga. The obsession heightened, at the beginning of her notoriety, when Lady Gaga wore elaborately bizarre costumes while performing. After graduating from high school, Kayvon attended college at Parsons School of Art and Design in New York City, majoring in fashion design. He loved to design couture and runway-style clothing. His signature style was elaborate clothing that involved a lot of leather, feathers, and outrageous headdresses. Not the type of clothing one would wear in the office. Hence, his obsession with the style that Lady Gaga donned in the early millennium.

During a bout of mania, Kayvon became convinced that Lady Gaga wanted to meet him. He obsessively followed her on Facebook and Twitter and informed me that she had contacted him and wanted him to design clothing for her. He bought a blond wig and dressed like her, parading around our home, singing her music. He videotaped himself during these performances and sent them to her via her fan website. I had to put my foot down when he told me she had contacted him and arranged to meet him in Times Square. Seriously?! When I refused to pay the bus fare, he retaliated by staging a protest. Unfortunately, his protest was staged, on the first day of school, down the middle of Main Street in front of the Galvin Middle School in Wakefield. Picture my son, dressed in a blond wig and self-designed gown, donning very bright red lipstick, marching down Main Street while hundreds of parents and students watched.

Fortunately, the Wakefield Police were quickly called to the scene. They diplomatically convinced him to leave. They loaded him in a cruiser, notified us, and suggested he get immediate psychiatric assistance. Sometimes, the best way to cope is to simply surrender to the hilarity of the situation.

Kayvon also is convinced that Google is spying on him. He believes this to be somewhat true even when he's not experiencing a manic or psychotic episode. When manic, Kayvon fears that Google can read his mind. He has gone to elaborate lengths to post warnings on social media concerning Google. He becomes convinced that Google is part of an evil empire that is gaining some sort of power by spying on us all and using the knowledge it gains to control the government. He ruminates and becomes convinced of a Google government conspiracy.

What we all understand is that Google, as a search engine, gathers information from our web searches and tailors that information to post advertising we may be interested in. Essentially Google is spying on us. However, while experiencing mania, Kayvon takes that knowledge and magnifies it in his mind. Many people who suffer from manic or psychotic episodes caused by bipolar disorder become obsessed with the government. This is often the reason one will learn about a mentally ill person who storms the post office or other government agencies. Psychosis causes a heightened sense of fear, paranoia, and mistrust. The mentally ill person often isn't held responsible for harmful, or even deadly actions due to the magnitude of the psychosis present at the time of the incident. They are found Not Guilty by Reason of Insanity.

During one episode of mania, Kayvon designed a sandwich board to wear in order to stage a protest against the evil empire Google. The costume underneath the sandwich board had hundreds of googly eyes glued to the sleeves and pants. The board read, *Warning: Google is spying on us all!* It featured a large, evil-eyed Google icon with a big X drawn through it. After his Google protest garb was complete, he requested that we drive him to McLean Hospital in Belmont, Massachusetts. He got out of the car, put on his anti-Google garb, and staged a singular protest in the McLean Hospital parking lot. While Kayvon was engaged in the protest, his father calmly walked into the admissions building and told them his son was having a psychiatric emergency. They inquired where his son was. Tom pointed to the parking lot and said, "That's him there." Two hospital aides were called down to greet Kayvon in the parking lot. Recognizing him immediately, the hospital aides calmly said, "Hi Kayvon, let's go inside." He was admitted to the McLean Hospital for a month of psychiatric help. Or, as Kayvon so fondly refers to it, *A Purgatory Vacation.*

CHAPTER FIVE

Birdman
(Not to Be Confused with the Michael Keaton film)

Another bizarre manic episode involved a made-up character that Kayvon constructed called Birdman. Kayvon loves to perform. He was the president of the drama club in high school and a very talented performer. He and his friends spent much of their spare time creating bizarre, yet creative and interesting videos. One film that they spent months creating involved this Birdman character. The video, filmed in the basement of a friend's home, was dark and disturbing. Birdman was a psychotic man who believed he was part bird/part man. His fingernails were grown long to resemble talons and had a beaklike face. Kayvon embraced this character, strutting around like a bird while making chirping sounds, while practicing at home. It was quite unusual but also amusing.

The summer following Kayvon's first year of college was a trying one. Kayvon struggles in the absence of structure, such as school, and has a difficult time focusing. This is due in part from his mental illness, but also because he has struggled since second grade with Attention Deficit Disorder. He was prescribed Ritalin during the school year but advised by his doctor to cease the medication during the summer. Kayvon got into a lot of trouble during the summer months without structure and his ADD medication. He often resorted to self-medicating with marijuana and alcohol. While on mood stabilizers to treat bipolar disorder, the combination of those two substances negated any therapeutic effect.

While we were away one summer night, unbeknownst to us, Kayvon decided to host a party at our home. He already was demonstrating hypomania and was beginning to spiral out of control. Of course, as any parent knows, an unsupervised party means trouble. We received a call from a neighbor late that evening informing us that the police were parked in front of our house. There were at least 50-100 teenagers, many of them heavily intoxicated, at our home being led down the driveway. We rushed home in the middle of the night.

We came home to discover our yard and home were trashed. Our gardens were torn to shreds, plants and large ceramic planters were thrown into our pool. The house had rooms with holes kicked in the walls and items thrown down the stairs were totally destroyed. Kayvon's sewing machines were in the bathtub floating in water. Talcum powder was sprayed everywhere. Light fixtures broken. Cans and bottles of alcohol were strewn everywhere. It was a disaster. Kayvon was nowhere to be found and wouldn't answer our calls. We were enraged and called the police. We figured that Kayvon had invited a few friends to the house and that the party grew as more kids found out about it. What we didn't know at the time was that Kayvon posted the party on Facebook and extended an open invitation to anyone who wanted to come.

The police took notes and inquired if we wished to press charges against our son since he was 19 years old and therefore technically responsible for the damage. We explained that he was experiencing hypomania and probably not of sound judgment. In retrospect, we should have pressed charges. Kayvon would've received a slap on the wrist and perhaps received the mental help he needed. Instead, we decided not to have him arrested and deal with the situation in our own way. Not a wise decision.

Kayvon hid from us for a couple of days, staying at his friends' houses and refusing to answer our calls. He knew we'd be furious and probably ground him or worse, kick him out. Of course, he also wasn't able to take his medication while away and was not sleeping. His hypomania quickly progressed into mania. He came home two days later. He was unkempt and unruly. He didn't apologize for hosting the party. He refused to give us any information regarding the damage. He simply stood in front of us, staring ahead, reciting an obscure poem over and over. He pushed past us, ignoring our questions while we argued with him. We were fed up and our anger escalated. We told him he needed to leave the house. He refused, ran to his room and locked the door.

Tom furiously knocked down the door and they got in a physical altercation. Neither of them were seriously injured, but tempers flared and Kayvon did leave the house. We had had enough. We were at our wits' end. The next day, at the suggestion of a relative in law enforcement, we went to court and took out a restraining order against our son. We needed a break from him.

A few days later, Kayvon showed up at our home insisting that he needed to gather some of his belongings. We informed him of the restraining order. He refused to leave. We called the police and told Kayvon the police were on their way. He ran up the stairs to his room and I followed him pleading with him to leave. He took a box cutter out of his pocket, pushed me against a wall and threatened to cut me. I screamed and tried to hide in the bathroom. He followed me, slammed the bathroom door shut and shoved me against the wall. Tom rescued me and the police arrived.

I wasn't present when the police finally found Kayvon. I was sitting on the bathroom floor, shaking while they chased him out of the woods surrounding our home and into a cruiser. A few years later, I heard from neighbors who witnessed the chase. They described the scene that ensued as heartbreaking. Kayvon was keening like a wild animal when the police finally found him. They had to use pepper spray and handcuffs to restrain him. When he passed a police vehicle containing a trained police dog, Kayvon began barking at the dog and taunting it. He was charged with assault and animal cruelty. He was held for trial and sent to Middlesex County Jail to serve time. Birdman saved Kayvon's life while serving time in jail.

The first month of incarceration, Kayvon refused our visits and phone calls. He hated us and blamed us. While incarcerated, inmates are able to receive their medication. Kayvon's moods began to stabilize once his medication levels became therapeutic. He wasn't receiving any psychotherapy. However, the structure of prison life coupled with the proper medication helped to bring his moods back to normal, thereby improving his cognitive function and behavior.

He eventually reached out to us by mail, requesting money for the canteen and that we send his Birdman script. Kayvon, a 19-year-old flamboyantly gay man, survived prison by entertaining the other prisoners. Can you just picture him: strutting like a bird, flapping his arms, and chirping while the other prisoners laughed hysterically? His Birdman character became notorious at that prison.

Birdman was a character that Kayvon embraced long after he was finally released from prison. One evening, while very manic, Kayvon called the Wakefield Police, requesting that he be taken to McLean Hospital. McLean Hospital was, and still is Kayvon's hospital of choice for treatment. Even while extremely manic, Kayvon possesses the ability to seek psychiatric help without our intervention. He has been treated at McLean Hospital several times and they know him well. He feels at home there.

That evening, while driving home from the gym, I rounded the corner to my street and saw blue and red lights flashing. Two police cruisers and fire trucks were parked in front of my home. I panicked, expecting the worse, parked my car, and ran up the sidewalk to my home. A police officer stopped me and warned me to stay back as this was a *family issue*. I informed the officer that it was my home and my family. He explained that my son had called them and asked to be taken away for psychiatric treatment. I heard a commotion and looked up. Coming out of my home, for the entire neighborhood to see, was Kayvon being escorted by two female police officers, one on each arm. He was stark naked, donning a pair of cowboy boots and his Birdman mask. He waved to me and yelled from behind his hideous bird mask, "Hi Mom! They're taking me to McLean Apple Farm." Sometimes, all you can do is laugh.

CHAPTER SIX

Social Media Sabotage

Kayvon can be cruel. This part of his illness is puzzling. For the past nine years since Kayvon received his diagnosis of bipolar disorder, his psychiatrists and therapists have wondered if he has another underlying psychiatric condition. When he was discharged from his most recent hospitalization, a diagnosis of *Borderline Personality Disorder* was mentioned. Unfortunately, this is a very difficult and tricky diagnosis to detect and nearly impossible to treat. There are no medications to treat a personality disorder. The treatment is intense behavior therapy. For the past few years, Kayvon has utilized many types of social media as a public forum to blackmail and sabotage people or organizations. He has written hurtful and embarrassing remarks with the intention of hurting friends, family members and strangers. The comments and remarks he has publicly shared have ruined reputations. His cyber bullying cost his brother TJ his job.

TJ was employed at a very well-known art gallery and entertainment venue in Cambridge. He was the manager and thoroughly loved his job. He often worked more than 80 hours a week, running events, scheduling exhibits and booking musical performances. The gallery's revenue often fell short, making it difficult to pay rent. TJ worked tirelessly, often without pay, to rally financial support for the gallery and was instrumental in making the gallery a nonprofit organization. TJ loved his job and the people who frequented the gallery. It was his life for three years.

One evening, everything went awry. A female vocalist who was scheduled to perform later in the evening began flirting with TJ. He flirted back, and they seemed to hit it off. After her performance, TJ congratulated her and tried to kiss her on the forehead. She freaked out. She ran out of the gallery quite upset. TJ was confused, yet also angry with himself for initiating the encounter. It was unprofessional and shouldn't have happened. He chastised himself and tried to find her to apologize. He couldn't find her that night.

The following day, the shit hit the fan. She posted an angry, angst-driven message on the art gallery website and tagged TJ and other co-workers at the gallery. She accused TJ of sexual assault. She exaggerated the incident and fabricated details of the encounter they had. An innocent kiss on the forehead became groping and assault. She accused the gallery of being an unsafe venue for female performers. She warned people to stay away. The post went viral.

Less than 12 hours after the incident allegedly occurred, TJ was fired from his job. He was devastated. His boss didn't listen or stand by him when he tried to explain that the entire incident was fabricated and the details grossly exaggerated. The owner of the gallery posted on the gallery's Facebook page that TJ was no longer welcome at the gallery. His position was terminated.

The enormity of this situation was unfathomable. Due to one false and fabricated post on social media, TJ lost his job and his reputation. Times like this are when one relies on family for emotional support and strength. Family and friends rallied to support him. They countered the posts on social media and stood by his side. We were all there for TJ. All except Kayvon.

The despicable post that Kayvon wrote on Facebook less than 24 hours after the notorious incident broke my heart. It was, and still is, unforgiveable. He described TJ as a deviant and a sexual predator who regularly molested Kayvon when he was young. He described, in detail, horrific acts that never occurred. Why? To get attention? To get back at his brother for something? Simply to be mean and vindictive? To this day, Kayvon and TJ do not speak.

Less than 24 hours later, the woman who accused TJ of sexual assault retracted her story. She posted on a personal blog that she had been a victim of sexual assault and rape in the past. She admitted that she exaggerated the details of the evening at the gallery and overreacted. She never pressed charges against TJ because nothing really happened. Too little, too late. The damage was done.

This incident of publicly shaming a family member wasn't a singular one. Kayvon has posted nasty and false comments about his sister. He's referred to her as *transphobic*. Once after I refused to give him money, Kayvon retaliated on Facebook by calling me *fake mom* and labeled me an *emotional abuser*. He even went as far as to post inexcusable remarks about his dead father. How do you forgive behavior like this?

I suppose there are many theories on why people engage in cyber bullying. I'm certain there are documented personality traits shared by people who cyber bully. What puzzles me is the reason why someone would intentionally burn bridges through public shaming. I have asked Kayvon why he does this. Does it make him feel better about himself to publicly hurt and shame others? Does he realize he is burning bridges and damaging relationships? Does he even care? He doesn't answer me. He doesn't appear to know the answer. The thing I grapple with is whether to forgive or simply accept. By accepting this personality trait of Kayvon's, am I enabling him to continue? Is this simply one of many frustrating and incomprehensible personality traits that are characteristics of his personality disorder? Should I feel sorry for his lack of remorse and common sense? While raising a child with mental illness, you must learn to accept but often make the decision of when to forgive.

CHAPTER SEVEN

The Looney Bin

Lonely. Desolate. Chaotic. Frightening. Gloomy. Loud. Extremely depressing. There are many words one could use to suitably depict a psychiatric facility and all of those words would apply. In the past 15 years, my sons have been admitted to nearly every psychiatric facility in Massachusetts. Each facility is similar. Some are worse than others. They can all be aptly described by using the above-mentioned adjectives. The atmosphere and physical set-up of a psychiatric facility cannot be compared to any other type of healthcare facility.

There are, however, common characteristics that psychiatric facilities share with other types of hospitals. They all offer care to patients who are sick. A vast majority of the patients being treated at any hospital may experience pain. The illnesses from which they are being treated are often chronic. Many patients will never be cured. And thankfully, both types of hospitals are staffed by competent and caring professionals. Yet, that is where the similarities end.

When you enter the lobby of a psychiatric facility, you are not greeted by a pleasant receptionist, sitting at an impressive information desk, who will happily validate your parking pass or direct you to your family member's floor. There are no gift shops containing balloons and flowers meant to brighten the patient's stay. There are no cafes or restaurants to visit while there. You don't take an elevator to the patient's assigned floor and simply walk into their room for a visit.

What is most remarkable about the lobby of a psychiatric facility is the lack of visible patients or visitors. The lobby is virtually empty except for a phone on the wall with instructions to call your family member's unit prior to visiting. The units are locked. Once on the floor of your family member's unit, you ring a bell to announce your arrival. You must be physically escorted to the patient's floor and unit. Your purse and pockets are checked for sharp objects or drugs. Your cell phone is confiscated. You are asked to remove your belt and sometimes your shoelaces. This is not a typical hospital. Welcome to the Looney Bin.

The door is unlocked, and you step inside. The atmosphere on these units is melancholy, yet at the same time, chaotic. Oftentimes, there are forlorn patients shuffling along the corridors, head downcast, mumbling. Sometimes, you'll hear screaming or hideous laughter. Patients are not wearing hospital-assigned Johnnies because those have ties. A patient may be able to commit suicide with any type of tie or string. Most patients wear old jeans or pants with elastic waists and slippers. Patients look disheveled and despondent, their hair uncombed and clothing soiled. Oftentimes, a pungent odor of urine mingled with sweat permeates the air.

Staff are often assigned to sit outside certain patient rooms to keep the patient from exiting his or her room. These are the most dangerously ill patients. The ones who may hurt someone, or if left alone, may hurt themselves. These rooms have no windows, a cot containing a mattress void of any bed linens in the middle of a stark room, and nothing else. Too much stimulus may exasperate the symptoms of these patients. These rooms contain the patients who are dangerously symptomatic with extreme psychosis and mania. They require a careful watch.

Every psychiatric facility that either TJ or Kayvon have spent time in is similar. Some facilities are worse than others. TJ has been hospitalized in countless facilities across the state of Massachusetts. I have lost track of how many, but I know he has been hospitalized more than 25 times since his initial diagnosis at age 17. He is currently 32. Both of my sons have been hospitalized at McLean Hospital and Bridgewater State Hospital. These facilities represent, in my opinion, the best and worst that the mental health system has to offer in the state of Massachusetts.

McLean Hospital is located in the well-to-do suburb of Belmont, just west of Boston. The hospital is situated on sprawling grounds referred to as the "McLean Hospital Campus." The stately buildings and manicured grounds actually do appear collegiate in this setting. The campus contains footpaths, ponds, and picnic areas that patients are allowed to use while supervised and when they are mentally stable enough to leave the locked units. The units that I have visited at McLean Hospital include sunny dining areas with windows in which to view the serene campus and living rooms equipped with TV's and board games. There are Art and Music Therapy rooms and rooms that contain gym equipment. Upon entering most units at this hospital, you'll see an elaborate and beautiful fish tank placed there to instill a sense of calm. Although the units are locked and the procedure for visiting the patient is stringent, McLean Hospital epitomizes the model of mental health care. It is a world-class mental health care facility.

Bridgewater State Hospital represents the polar opposite in mental healthcare. Driving down the desolate road to this state facility, passing by several buildings that house prisoners, you eventually come upon the Bridgewater State Prison. The buildings and parking lots are surrounded by barbed wire and electric security fences. I'll never forget my first visit to Bridgewater State Hospital. I was chilled by the foreboding atmosphere. I recall seeing prisoners wearing orange jumpsuits playing basketball in courts encased in barbed wire as I drove to the hospital at the end of the road. I couldn't believe that my son was actually being held in a facility located within the state prison system for mental health treatment.

I was naïve and ill prepared for what was to be the first of many visits to Bridgewater State Hospital. Little did I know that jewelry of any kind was not allowed inside the facility. I had to leave all my jewelry, including my wedding ring, in my car. I took a number and lined up along with several other visitors who were anxiously waiting to be called by a uniformed guard located behind a glass window. Once I submitted the necessary paperwork to the guard, my son's cellblock was notified that he had a visitor. He would then be escorted to a common visiting room along with all the other patients for a 30-minute visit in a room surrounded by guards. Before entering the visiting room, I had to be searched. I had to take off my shoes and was patted down. They lifted the hair on the back of my neck and looked in my mouth to check for contraband. I had to walk through an electronic security gate containing a metal detector. On one occasion, I was strip searched because my underwire bra set off the metal detector. It is humiliating and unimaginable that this facility is considered to be a mental health treatment center. Not only are the patients treated like prisoners, but their family and friends are made to feel like criminals as well.

I remember seeing my son, wearing an orange jumpsuit, lined up waiting to be escorted in to the crowded and chaotic visiting room. Once inside, he hugged me but was warned of no physical contact by the guards. He appeared frightened and was heavily medicated, slurring his words and drooling. He convinced me that he was receiving his mood stabilizers and assured me that he was OK. I had my doubts. He has later confessed that he often saw other patients being assaulted and taunted while housed in this facility. He received little or no treatment in the form of psychotherapy by a licensed therapist. He was only allowed to attend AA meetings held inside the facility. He spent most of this time playing cards. He was not allowed outside in the fenced-in yard. It ended up being an arduous and frustrating six-week hospitalization.

Bridgewater State Hospital serves as a "holding tank" for those who commit crimes while manic or psychotic, oftentimes of a violent nature, yet are deemed by the court system to be "not competent to stand trial." The patients are there because they are mentally ill. Most have been accused of a crime yet not formally tried. TJ was housed in that facility along with sexual deviants, murderers, drug dealers, and men accused of assault. The common factor among all of these men was that they were waiting to stand trial. They were innocent until proven guilty. Yet, they were locked in cells, forced to survive on unhealthy and tasteless food, while receiving minimal mental help. They were all mentally ill but treated like animals. Bridgewater State Hospital is not the looney bin. It is a zoo.

CHAPTER EIGHT

Welcome Aboard the Bipolar Express

I'll never forget my first experience inside a psychiatric facility. My older son TJ had been transported by ambulance to Arbour-Fuller Hospital in South Attleboro, MA the night before. It was his first psychiatric hospitalization. He was 17 years old. He had spent the night in the emergency unit of Melrose-Wakefield hospital for psychiatric evaluation. He was deemed a danger to himself and others. He was transported to South Attleboro on a stretcher in four-point restraints (leather straps attached to the stretcher restraining his legs and arms) while heavily sedated with injections of Haldol and Ativan. These drugs are considered chemical restraints used to tranquilize a patient who is out of control. It was the worst night of my life. This night marked the beginning of a long, arduous journey.

I can still recall the visceral feeling of cold that invaded my body that evening. It was a seasonal spring evening yet the memories from that night still give me the chills. The sense of desperation and confusion I felt when I first received the news that something was wrong with my son is still palatable.

I had just returned home from teaching a group exercise class when I received the phone call from my friend and neighbor, Chris. She said something was wrong with TJ. His friends were worried about his erratic and frightening behavior. He took some kind of drugs, jumped out of their car while they were driving him home, and ran. They found him walking next to the railroad tracks and talked him into coming to her house. He was at her house now but was out of control. TJ was desperate and frantic, punching and kicking her husband while he was trying to calm TJ down.

"Joie, I think TJ is having some sort of mental breakdown," Chris said. "I believe he needs psychiatric help." This would mark the first of more than 25 psychiatric hospitalizations for TJ in only 12 years.

That evening, I called my brother-in-law Matt, a police officer who served in a nearby community. He agreed to meet TJ at Chris's house. Matt had professional training in dealing with individuals who may be experiencing a psychiatric emergency. We also figured that as TJ's uncle, Matt would appear less threatening than a uniformed police officer arriving in a police cruiser. Matt arrived at our neighbor's home in plainclothes driving the family van. After a brief meeting with TJ, he called us and told us he was driving TJ to the nearest emergency room for evaluation. He asked that we meet them at the hospital instead of accompanying them.

I remember entering the room in the emergency unit at Melrose-Wakefield Hospital where TJ was being evaluated. Before I entered the room, I was greeted by a heavy-set and intimidating uniformed guard who was guarding TJ's room. This was the first time I laid eyes on TJ that evening. He was pacing around the room, wild-eyed, and highly agitated. He was mumbling nonsensical and outlandish gibberish about solving the Theory of PI. He wanted to leave and insisted nothing was wrong. He argued that we were the ones who had something wrong with us.

I can still feel the chill from the cold vinyl couch that I sat on and the assault of the blinding lights overhead while waiting for an answer. It was surreal. I felt as if I was living in a nightmare. What was happening to make my son act in such a bizarre manner? Was it drug related? A brain tumor?

Finally, after what appeared to be an eternity of waiting, a nurse came in to inform me that TJ had been blood screened and drug-tested and that they were waiting for the results. She also told me that a social worker from a local mental health emergency team would be coming as soon as possible to evaluate TJ. The long and arduous wait for answers ensued. It seemed like hours before someone came in to check in on us or give us any information. During that time, TJ grew more agitated and extremely belligerent. He yelled at the security guard to let him out. He ranted about the "establishment" and how he was the second savior like Jesus Christ. He could not stop talking. He couldn't sit still.

The mental health counselor who came to evaluate TJ was an attractive woman in her mid-20s. She was the first kind person I saw that evening, yet probably not the most appropriate choice for evaluating a manic 17-year-old. I was appalled by TJ's behavior toward her. My typically shy and polite son began asking her if she'd go to bed with him while making rude and inappropriately sexual comments about her appearance. I kept insisting that TJ stop. It was humiliating. She turned to me and calmly explained that TJ probably couldn't stop. She told me that a characteristic of mania, caused by a potential mental illness, is hypersexuality. TJ was clearly manic.

I would later learn about many of the other characteristics of mania that were exhibited by TJ that evening. TJ could not stop talking. While interviewing TJ, the female counselor requested that he stop talking and simply listen to her for a minute. She pointed to the clock on the wall and asked him to look at the clock. She asked him to wait one full minute while simply listening to her before vocalizing. He could not. She kept lessening the time, first to 30 seconds and then to 10 seconds. He talked incessantly and was not able to wait a mere five seconds before ranting and raving about sex, the Theory of PI, the establishment, or Jesus Christ. She turned to me and told me TJ's speech was "pressured," another characteristic of mania.

She also asked TJ to explain to her how he solved the Theory of PI or 3.14. I can't remember the conversation and to me it was simply nonsense. To TJ, this was reality. He honestly believed he was so brilliant that he possessed the ability to solve a complicated mathematical theory on his own. TJ was "grandiose," another characteristic of mania. While manic, many people with mental illness will experience a feeling of euphoria that leads them to believe they are more intelligent, artistic, and stronger than the average human being. Grandiosity can be exhilarating and powerful. Musicians, poets, and artists who are bipolar often create their most celebrated forms of art while grandiose.

Because TJ had exhibited many of the characteristics and symptoms of mania and psychosis, the counselor recommended that he be hospitalized. She told him that he would need to be placed in a psychiatric facility for his own safety and the safety of others. It was there that he would receive the medications and psychiatric treatment necessary to stabilize his moods. She told us she needed to make some calls for placement and that it may take some time, so we should simply wait. That's when TJ panicked, and all hell broke loose.

As soon as the counselor left the room TJ bolted, running out of the room and down the corridor trying to escape. I remember the security guard yelling at him to stop and calling for back-up on his walkie talkie as he began chasing TJ. I heard a code being initiated over the hospital intercom. The police were notified, and the chase began. TJ was eventually caught after wrestling and injuring a few hospital security guards and police officers. He was out of control and deemed a danger to himself and others. He was involuntarily committed for 72 hours of observation in a psychiatric facility. An involuntary commitment is officially known as a "Section 12" in the state of Massachusetts. It's also known as being "pink-slipped." TJ was given his first ticket aboard the Bipolar Express.

CHAPTER NINE

First Stop: South Attleboro

The feeling of dread and disbelief that a parent of a child who is first diagnosed with a chronic mental illness feels is indescribable. There is no easy way to tell a parent that their child may live a life that will be extremely difficult, confusing, challenging and misunderstood. I felt like all my dreams, hopes, and desires for my son's future had come to a halting stop. There is no way to console a parent who is grieving a life that would be lost.

There are medications that will manage the symptoms or stabilize the moods, but none that will cure the disease. To make matters worse, the medications, when used over a period of time, often cause havoc with the liver and may eventually leave the patient with potentially dangerous physical symptoms. The medications used to manage symptoms often make the patient feel lethargic, flat, and zombie-like. Many of the mood stabilizers used to manage depression, psychosis, or a bipolar disorder also cause significant weight gain. Frankly, the lifelong challenge of managing mental illness is to keep the patient medicated. The symptoms of the illness, such as grandiosity, euphoria, heightened creativity, and the ability to stay awake and alert for days without sleep are all so much more provocative than the negative side effects caused by the medications used to control the symptoms.

What happened when TJ opened his eyes and saw us there broke my heart. He could barely speak, as if his tongue was too big for his mouth. He tried to speak but his speech was so slurred from the medications used to sedate him that it was nearly impossible to understand him. He became frustrated that we couldn't understand him. He grew more and more agitated when he kept repeating himself. His agitation fueled what happened next.

As quick as a shot from a cannon, TJ jumped up, grabbed my purse and ran. He flew out of his room and raced at a lightning pace down the corridor. We stood in his room dumbfounded. What the hell? Nurses and security guards began chasing him. No one could catch him. A code was initiated throughout the hospital, alerting all personnel to TJ's unit. We heard doors being locked and lights within the unit began flashing. The hospital was in the middle of a psychiatric emergency. The emergency was my son.

When things finally settled down, a nurse found us and told us that it would be necessary for TJ to be physically and chemically restrained. He was out of control. She suggested that we go home because it may be awhile before he would be back in his room and that he was in no condition for visitors. I was devastated, confused, and angry that we had driven so far to only lay eyes on TJ for less than 15 minutes. The nurse sensed my frustration and told me she would ask the psychiatrist who was treating TJ to speak to us before we left. Finally, I was going to get an explanation for the bizarre behavior exhibited by my son in the past 24 hours.

The news I received that day was not what I wanted to hear. Results from the blood screens taken at the emergency room the night before, showed that he had smoked pot, drank alcohol, and ingested some other substance that was not as easy to detect. Perhaps an opioid of some sort? The doctor explained that this trace opioid may have been laced in the pot. He told us that these substances most likely weren't the cause of TJ's erratic behavior although they may have exasperated his symptoms. In his opinion, TJ was experiencing symptoms of mania and psychosis. He told us that TJ's diagnosis was Bipolar Disorder.

The doctor delivered this news in a frank yet sympathetic manner. He told us that he was sorry to tell us this. He told us that most males who were diagnosed with any type of mental illness were diagnosed while in their late teens or early 20's. He said that the behavior that TJ was displaying represented the classic symptoms of bipolar disorder. In order to keep this chronic illness under control, TJ would likely endure a lifetime of medication and psychotherapy.

When TJ was discharged from Arbour Hospital in South Attleboro, he was only 17 years old. TJ had to wait four weeks for a follow-up psychiatric appointment. During that time, he was taking the medications prescribed to him upon discharge. The combination of lithium and thorazine made TJ drowsy and appear zombie-like. He returned to high school and had to visit the nurse's office during the school day to take his midday medication. It was heartbreaking to see the change in his demeanor. And it must have been difficult for TJ to get through the school day.

His first psychiatrist office was conveniently located close to our home. Since TJ was a new patient, he had to undergo an intake psychiatric appointment that included a lengthy list of questions pertaining to TJ's medical history. During that appointment, the psychiatrist reviewed the hospital notes, paused, looked up at us, and told us that he was skeptical of TJ's diagnosis. He told us that many young adult males who are initially diagnosed with Bipolar Disorder are often misdiagnosed. He felt that TJ may have appeared manic since he was admitted to the hospital while under the influence of alcohol, marijuana and opiates. He also informed us that testosterone levels in young adult males can dramatically affect moods. At 17, TJ was considered very young to be positively diagnosed with a serious mood disorder. He suggested that TJ may not need to be medicated with such potent mood stabilizers. He felt that TJ simply needed to be treated with psychotherapy to deal with his substance abuse. He was wrong.

CHAPTER TEN

The Challenge of New Medications

I don't have any medical experience. I'm not qualified to spew the science behind the mood stabilizers or anti-psychotics that are prescribed for treating mood disorders. I don't even fully comprehend the efficacy behind these medications. However, I am a mother of two sons who have both been prescribed a variety of mood stabilizers and anti-psychotics over the course of several years. I know that the medications work, but only if they are taken religiously. I am fully aware that most of these medications are all very expensive. I also have experienced firsthand how alcohol and other substances will lessen the effectiveness of these medications.

Although there are medications that will manage the symptoms or stabilize the moods, none will cure the disease. To make matters worse, these medications, when used over a period of time, often cause havoc with the liver and may eventually leave the patient with potentially dangerous physical symptoms. The medications used to manage symptoms often make the patient feel lethargic, flat, and zombie-like. Many of the mood stabilizers used to manage depression, psychosis, or bipolar disorder also cause significant weight gain.

Frankly, the lifelong challenge of managing mental illness is to keep the patient medicated. Symptoms of the illness such as grandiosity, euphoria, heightened creativity, and the ability to stay awake and alert for days without sleep are all so much more provocative than the negative side effects caused by the medications used to control the symptoms.

Since his first diagnosis, TJ was hospitalized more than 25 times between ages 17-29. The majority of these hospitalizations occurred due to his continued reluctance to stay on his medications. He fought his meds tooth and nail. He hated the side effects caused by taking lithium used to stabilize his moods. His hands shook, he gained weight and he felt thirsty all the time.

During his childhood and early teens, TJ was always considered a big boy. While growing up, he was often described as a teddy bear. Large, yet sweet and docile. He always struggled with his weight but was never actually obese. He was active and played football, baseball, and basketball in all the local youth sports teams. Often while taking Zyprexa, a long-term anti-psychotic, TJ will gain up to 50 pounds in a few short weeks. His appetite becomes relentless while taking this anti-psychotic.

Other medications, such as the ones used to control the more acute and severe psychosis caused by mania, have side effects that are far worse. In the past, Thorazine has been used to lessen the symptoms of TJ's psychosis. Thorazine, a tried and true anti-psychotic, debilitates motor skills and impairs speech. These side effects are more pronounced, but thankfully short lived since Thorazine isn't used for an extended period.

While taking Thorazine, TJ would shuffle his feet while walking, often referred as "The Thorazine Shuffle." His motor skills become so dramatically impaired while on Thorazine that he has difficulty feeding himself. It was extremely disturbing and pathetic to witness the lack of coordination that results from this medication. I remember visiting TJ on one occasion while hospitalized at McLean Hospital and finding him in his room trying to eat peanut butter with a toothbrush. Other times, he has had to be spoon-fed by a nurse or an aide.

While hospitalized, patients are not allowed to have cell phones. In most psychiatric units, there are a few pay phones for patients to use to in order to make outside calls to family or friends. Often the patients will stand in line for several minutes while waiting for their turn. It was heartbreaking when TJ would call home because it was nearly impossible for me to understand anything he was trying to say. He would grow more and more impatient and frustrated trying to repeat himself and often bang the receiver against the wall in distress.

As with TJ, many people with mental illness will often discontinue their meds once they become stable. After a few months or even years, the lure of living a life free from the side effects caused by mood stabilizers is enticing and impossible to resist. As time goes by, it becomes easier and easier to forget the most recent hospitalization. A false sense of security ensues, and medications are skipped or forgotten altogether. It often takes several hospitalizations and years of therapy for a mentally ill person to succumb to the fact that being med-compliant is the predominant way to remain stable. After more than 25 hospitalizations lasting the course of 15 years, I think TJ is finally catching on.

CHAPTER ELEVEN

Dual Diagnosis

TJ is extremely intelligent and a gifted artist and musician. His first hospitalization happened during the spring of his junior year of high school. He was enrolled in college-level, advanced placement classes during his junior and senior years. He missed nearly a month of school due to his initial diagnosis and treatment for bipolar disorder. Despite that, TJ would still graduate in the top 10 percent of his graduating class.

TJ applied for admission to several colleges such as Berklee College of Music, Roger Williams University, and Northeastern University. He was accepted at all of them, yet never attended any. TJ's struggles with his moods led him to self-medicate with alcohol and drugs.

I should've seen the signs that my son was struggling with alcoholism and drug abuse long before I actually did. If you ask TJ today when he first began drinking, he'd tell you that he remembers sneaking alcohol in middle school. He once confessed that he began having trouble sleeping as early as fifth grade. He told me he'd get up in the middle of the night and raid the medicine cabinet to ingest cold and cough medication by the mouthfuls. TJ's mind raced at night causing insomnia at an early age. Could TJ's insomnia have been an early signal of the onset of bipolar disorder? I'm not sure. I don't think anyone could tell us when his symptoms actually began. However, his addiction to alcohol and drugs most likely began when TJ started self-medicating at age 11.

Parents are warned to look for signs of substance abuse in their teenagers. I recall a popular commercial shown on television in the late 1990's. It depicted an egg being fried in a skillet with the caption reading, "This is your brain. This is your brain on drugs." I recall reading about the warning signals to look for in your teenage child, including a change in friends, mood swings, a lack of interest in activities such as clubs, sports, school, and sleeping too much. Any number of these signs may indicate substance abuse or depression. By his sophomore year of high school, TJ demonstrated several, if not all, of these warning signs. His large circle of friends, who typically included members of his football or basketball teams, dwindled to one or two. He quit the football team. He had difficulty getting up in time for school and often had to attend Saturday detention due to his constant tardiness. He constantly argued with us and seemed angry all the time. We simply chalked his change in behavior to teenage angst. Don't all teenagers rebel against their parents?

The anomaly of the situation was that TJ was able to maintain status quo. Even though we wondered whether TJ was doing OK, it was easy to dismiss the subtle yet noticeable changes in his behavior. He was able to maintain his studies and keep up his grades in Advanced Placement level classes, all while holding down a job. He was inducted into the National Honor Society in his junior year of High School. We were convinced that TJ would grow eventually out of this rebellious adolescent behavior.

Ultimately, it became more and more difficult for TJ to hide his secrets. He began getting into numerous automobile accidents, running red lights, going through stop signs and speeding. His first arrest occurred with a group of friends who decided it would be comical to drive around the local lake and shoot a BB gun at pedestrians. He lost a job. He stayed out many evenings, telling us he was sleeping over at various friends' houses. When he returned home, he would sleep all day. Little did we realize that his substance abuse was spiraling out of control. Later, we would learn that TJ was self-medicating. He was desperately trying to quiet his restless mind.

At some point during TJ's sophomore year of high school, my husband and I agreed that we should call a therapist. We arranged an appointment for family therapy. TJ was growing more and more distant and sleeping way too much. We worried that this was not typical behavior and wondered if he may be suffering from depression. TJ agreed to attend therapy with us. It didn't go well.

I don't recall what was said during the meeting with the therapist, but I do remember that TJ didn't utter one word. I remember being extremely frustrated with him. The therapist asked him several questions and he would literally ignore her or simply stare at her in a hostile manner. At one point, I insisted that he was being rude and implored that he answer her. She turned to me and said, "By TJ not talking, he is speaking volumes." She then addressed us, ignoring TJ, and told us she thought that TJ may be suffering from clinical depression and may benefit from antidepressants. TJ refused. Thankfully. We now realize that if TJ had agreed to take an antidepressant, his mania would have been exasperated. Within a year, TJ's depression waned and his mania mushroomed. During that year, TJ would regularly self-medicate with marijuana, alcohol, crack cocaine, and LSD.

My worst fears were soon confirmed when I began noticing that the alcohol in our house began disappearing. JoEllen was attending college and was no longer living at home. Kayvon was too young. I remember looking for signs that TJ was stealing our alcohol by looking under his bed when he was out. What I found shocked and saddened me. His room was littered with empty beer bottles and cans that were strewn under his bed or in his closet. During further investigation, I found bags of pot and devices such as pipes and bongs hidden among his belongings. The evidence confirming his substance abuse was hidden everywhere. We did what all parents do, we threatened him, grounded him, and told him we were concerned and disappointed. In the end, it didn't matter. He was already addicted to alcohol. He was only 16.

By the time TJ was first hospitalized at age 17, he would regularly abuse many other types of drugs. The following three years while TJ still lived in our home, I must have searched his room for evidence at least once a week. I remember finding small, quarter-size bags hidden in between his mattress. I didn't know what they were. I also found homemade devices that TJ used to smoke cocaine. I had no idea what these bags may have contained, yet I never confronted TJ about these items. What was I afraid of?

To this day, I'm not even sure why I conducted my weekly search of TJ's room. In order to gain control over a situation I had no control of? To prove that my suspicions were valid? To have concrete evidence that I could someday use against him? I still don't have an answer to why I did this yet didn't do anything about it.

Those three years were a nightmare. During my weekly searches, I discovered that TJ was not taking his mood stabilizers. I would often find piles of Lithium, Depakote, and Zyprexa strewn under his bed. Eventually, as the therapeutic effect of the mood stabilizers dissolved from his system, he would require hospitalization. It became a relentless cycle of depression, self-medication, mania, psychosis, noncompliance to medication, and more self-medication resulting into further hospitalization.

TJ admitted several years later, that those bags I found in his room had contained crack cocaine, ecstasy, or LSD. He recently admitted that the only drug he didn't use during those tumultuous three years was heroin. We are all thankful for that. He probably would be dead today.

Each time TJ was admitted to a psychiatric facility during those three years, he would be drug tested upon arrival. He always tested positive. Whether it was alcohol, marijuana, cocaine, ecstasy, or LSD, it really didn't matter. What mattered was that TJ's diagnosis became more complicated and more difficult to treat. He suffered from bipolar disorder and substance abuse. Like many people who suffer from some type of mental illness, TJ was dual diagnosed.

I admit it. During those tumultuous three years when TJ was abusing multiple illegal substances and not med compliant, I did some crazy things to "take control" of the uncontrollable. Room searches were the norm. Yet, when I look back at those years, I remember doing some pretty abnormal things myself, such as sneaking Ativan into his scrambled eggs.

Back then, in the early years of his diagnosis, TJ would send subtle signals that indicated that he was losing control. To this day, he still demonstrates similar behaviors. When TJ initially begins to slip into mania, he demonstrates signs of OCD, or Obsessive-Compulsive Disorder. He'll compulsively and continuously wash his hands. He'll scrub them so often and with such conviction they become red and raw. He obsessively cleans his living space. He'll stay up all night cleaning and reorganizing his room and now his apartment. To this day, if TJ tells me he's been doing a little "spring cleaning" I get nervous about his mental health.

Another sign that TJ may be nonmed-compliant is that he'll lose a significant amount of weight. I've mentioned that the mood stabilizers used to treat bipolar disorder typically cause weight gain. Once the mood stabilizers dissipate from his blood stream, TJ becomes more energetic as the extra pounds melt away. In the past, while still living at home, he'd wake me up in the middle of the night to tell me he was going for a run.

All of these signs indicate that TJ is becoming hypomanic, the preliminary stage of mania. This stage is a glorious and elegant feeling for someone with bipolar disorder. The newfound energy fuels all sorts of accomplishments that are often difficult when someone feels lethargic and sluggish from the effect of the mood stabilizers. They feel more creative, productive, happy, and satisfied with life than they typically do. The feeling is alluring and addictive. The problem is that hypomania doesn't last long. TJ once described the feeling of hypomania as "standing on the edge of the ocean and watching the tide come, in awe of its beauty, yet fully aware that a huge wave is going to knock you off your feet." Very soon, within days, the wave would come in, knock TJ off his feet, and he'd slip into full-blown mania and psychosis.

Another very idiosyncratic sign that TJ is slipping mentally is that he starts to obsessively consume eggs. He'll consume them in such large quantities that they become his single food source for days. On more than one occasion, I decided as a last-ditch effort for sanity, that it may be a good idea to slip some Ativan into his scrambled eggs. I was desperate for some resolve. While preparing his scrambled eggs, I'd crush some Ativan (probably more than I should have) into the mix. I did this a lot. Did it help? Not really. In the end, he'd still end up in the emergency room of some local hospital with full-scale mania waiting for a bed in a psychiatric facility. I remember on one occasion while admitting TJ for psychiatric treatment, answering several questions posed by the emergency room physician. She inquired about his medications and compliance. TJ was sitting in front of me quite agitated. I told her about his mood stabilizers and that he probably hadn't taken them for weeks. She asked TJ if he had taken anything else. He answered that he had not, even though it was a lie. That's when I piped in and told her I had been sneaking Ativan into his scrambled eggs. I remember the incredulous look on both of their faces. The doctor just shook her head. TJ turned to me and asked, "Really, Mom? Why the hell did you do that?"

The answer is that it made me feel better. Spiking TJ's eggs with Ativan gave me some sense of power. Why? It's difficult to explain and even more difficult to imagine, the experience of living with someone who's sliding into mania. Residing with a mentally ill person who has uncontrolled symptoms of mental illness is loud, intrusive, frightening, frustrating, and often shocking. You experience a roller coaster of emotions that can vacillate from feeling sorry for this person to wishing they would leave you alone. You feel sad, angry, frustrated, and most prominently, powerless.

I've been saddened by the enormity of how mental illness has stolen my sons' personalities and changed their lives. I've been frustrated when they chose to not take their medications and/or self-medicate with drugs and alcohol. I'm often angry that my sons' lives will be forever changed due to mental illness. But the emotion I've felt most often is helpless because I have absolutely no power over their mental illness.

The scrambled eggs and Ativan didn't help to keep TJ's mania at bay. It may have calmed him down a little, but only temporarily. Don't judge me. That simple, yet illogical act made me feel better at the time. I felt like I was doing something. And during those times, fraught with turmoil and confusion, doing something felt better than doing nothing.

CHAPTER TWELVE
The Same Yet Entirely Different

Mental illness is scary. You've seen the crazy person, talking to himself or herself, babbling nonsensically or ranting and raving like a lunatic in public places. The person you avoid making eye contact with. The person you steer clear of. Imagine that person is your child, husband, wife, mother, father, sister or brother. And try to keep in mind that that person is not responsible for their actions. A symptomatic mentally ill person is someone who is suffering. It's not easy to look mental illness in the face because it's alarming to witness a person in the depths of psychosis.

Many of TJ's most bizarre incidents while suffering from psychosis also could be described as fascinating. I don't want to mislead you into believing that I ever enjoyed witnessing the mayhem that has occurred when TJ was psychotic. That's far from the truth. It's like watching a runaway train. You can't believe it's happening. You know it's not going to end well. Yet, you can't take your eyes off its power, speed, and strength.

Kayvon's mania differs from TJ's mania. Kayvon's mania is grandiose, flamboyant, and often comical. TJ's mania is loud, disruptive, alarming, and often dangerous. Kayvon believes his outlandish and eccentric behavior to be nothing out of the ordinary. He tends to go to extreme measures to draw attention to himself while making poor and inappropriate decisions.

TJ, on the other hand, hides in fear when his mania and psychosis takes control of his mind. He becomes convinced that a government agency is watching him. He runs, hides, and panics. I've often found TJ barricaded behind his bedroom door, with the shades drawn, convinced that the CIA or the FBI were hunting him down.

Other times TJ has left the house dressed in army fatigues, armed with a backpack containing a paintball gun, trolling the subways and streets of Boston in search of his imaginary assailants. In the past, I've called the Boston Police and the MBTA to warn them; giving them a full description of my son. I've pleaded with the police to find him and bring him to an emergency room for psychiatric intervention. I've often been worried about what TJ is capable of doing when he becomes this paranoid.

Kayvon on the other hand, has been watched by the FBI for years. Since the incident at the Boston Marathon finish line, Kayvon has been placed on a FBI Terrorism Watch list. The night of the incident, the FBI confiscated his laptop and discovered disturbing posts that glamorized the actual surviving Marathon bomber, Dzhokhar Tsarnaev. Since then, Kayvon's activities and social media posts have been closely scrutinized by the FBI. I actually had an FBI agent contact me within the past year. He tried contacting my cell phone and when I didn't answer because I didn't know who was calling, he came to my residence and left his business card. On the business card, he wrote a note instructing me to contact him as soon as possible. When I contacted him, he asked where Kayvon was now living and told me it was very important that I provide him with Kayvon's most recent address. He warned me that he would find Kayvon, even if it meant making a visit to his place of employment.

Apparently Kayvon had posted a picture of then presidential candidate Donald Trump with the caption "Bomb the Whitehouse." As one would expect, the FBI took this very seriously. Kayvon, not so much.

TJ's paranoia during times of psychosis and mania is frightening and sad. It's frightening to observe the magnitude of fear and confusion brought on by delusional thoughts. I recall driving TJ to an event in Boston in my convertible. He asked that I drive him to meet his friends instead of taking a bus or a train. It was a lovely summer evening, yet TJ was clearly experiencing a psychotic episode. He was argumentative and agitated. He told me he was afraid to take public transportation because people were after him. I tried to convince him otherwise and he grew more agitated and began yelling at me. When I asked him to calm down, he literally jumped out of my convertible in the middle of Storrow Drive, a very busy thoroughfare that parallels the Charles River in Boston, and ran into traffic. I'm surprised he wasn't killed.

The similarities of their illnesses are fascinating. Both of my sons obsess over numbers when they begin to slip into mania. I've been informed that this a classic symptom displayed in anyone who is bipolar. Numbers help the mentally ill organize their disordered and cluttered minds. TJ, while at the brink of psychosis, obsesses over the Theory of PI or 3.14. Kayvon becomes consumed by numerology, or the numbers and patterns created in one's name. During an early manic episode, Kayvon went to the extreme of having the numerological table permanently tattooed to his wrist.

Also, typical of anyone who is manic, both sons stop eating and sleeping for days. I have been alarmed and astonished by the amount of time TJ and Kayvon could stay awake and extremely alert without sleep during manic episodes. This manic insomnia coupled with a lack of food fueled the psychosis that would eventually follow.

Both of my sons become very hypersexual during bouts of mania. Although this characteristic is similar for both of them, it is displayed in two distinct manners. I recall visiting TJ at a psychiatric facility and upon entering his room, I was shocked that the entire wall was decorated with magazine pictures of young women dressed in exercise attire. I suppose it could have been worse. I should've been thankful that more risqué magazines weren't available on the psych unit.

Kayvon's hypersexuality, characteristic of his typically extravagant behavior while manic, is far more dramatic. Once, during a visit to McLean Hospital, Kayvon pulled down his pants and exposed himself to me and anyone else who was lingering in the corridor. Another time, while he was hospitalized, I received a phone call from a nurse on duty notifying me of an incident that had occurred between Kayvon and another male patient. I remember the conversation because it was actually quite comical. The nurse who called me told me she had good news and bad news. The good news was that Kayvon's thoughts were becoming more organized, a sign that his mania was abating. The bad news was that he, along with another male patient, developed an elaborate plan to "sneak by the aides on duty" and meet for a brief sexual rendezvous in the shower. This was definitely against hospital protocol.

TJ and Kayvon's addiction to cigarette smoking also is a prevalent trait they both share. This irks me because their father succumbed to head and neck cancer, a disease that was most likely caused from his habit of smoking cigarettes. Both sons bore witness to their father's one-year battle, suffering through chemotherapy, radiation, a tracheostomy, and a feeding tube. One would think that the obvious choice would be to quit smoking. Yet, they both smoke at least a pack a day. While hospitalized, neither of them are able to smoke. Many of their hospitalizations last six weeks or longer. At that point, their bodies undergo complete nicotine withdrawal. Yet, both sons, as soon as they are discharged from the hospital, will race to the store to purchase cigarettes. I find this infuriating at times, but as a parent of a child who is mentally ill, you have to learn to choose your battles. In the grand scheme of things, smoking cigarettes, albeit detrimental to their physical health, must be overlooked. As with many who are mentally ill, smoking is considered calming and pleasurable. And if one has a mood disorder, ingesting anything legal that brings a sense of comfort and a heightened mood is a good thing.

Both of my sons have gained a significant amount of weight due to their mood stabilizers and antipsychotics. Over the years, they have each fought this side effect in a similar manner: refusing to take a recommended medication, trying alternatives types of mood stabilizers that have less tendency toward weight gain, or stopping medication altogether. Most of these tactics have worked for a short period of time. Short term weight loss has resulted, but within 6-8 weeks, this weight loss is typically followed by a long-term hospitalization.

Unfortunately, a common thread they both share when manic is an enormous amount of anger. The anger is often directed at me. This display of anger can be cruel and often quite alarming. I've been informed that it's typical for a manic person to display anger toward the people whom they care the most for. That may be true but it's still hurtful. They argue, pick fights, and say things that can be painful to hear. TJ can get physically aggressive while angry. Past manic episodes have resulted in physical altercations with close friends and dangerous fights with his father. He's also pushed me, threatened me, and screamed obscenities. Once, while driving on the highway just after a premature discharge from the hospital, TJ became very agitated. He kept telling me to drive faster and insisted that I increase the volume on my radio to a deafening level. I suggested that he may've been discharged from the hospital too early and told him to calm down or I'd turn the car around at the next exit and bring him back to be admitted again. He reached over and grabbed my steering wheel in an attempt to take control of the car and could have killed us both.

Kayvon picks verbal fights. He becomes mean and spiteful. His anger also is threatening, but not in a physical manner. When Kayvon's manic anger rages, he takes enormous effort to entertain arguments. As one of his therapists noted, "Kayvon tries to draw you into his web of rage and anger. The best thing to do is to let him rant, but not to participate. Don't get caught in his web. You'll never win." It takes every ounce of control to not engage in his wrath. The things he says or posts on social media while enraged are vengeful and despicable. Over the years, he has burned many bridges.

Both of my sons have been diagnosed with the same illness. They each express symptoms that are considered classic for people living with bipolar disorder. At the same time, the way these symptoms are expressed is often quite unique for each of them. Showing the distinctions between the two of them is my way of painting a picture for you.

When my sons were younger, at the beginning of this journey, I was told that the majority of people who are diagnosed with bipolar disorder will someday attempt suicide. That was a scary thing to hear and difficult to imagine at the time. Thankfully, the other similar characteristic that both my sons share is that they've each promised me that they would never kill themselves. There is hope.

CHAPTER THIRTEEN

Riding on the Double Decker

It happened about five years after TJ's initial diagnosis. At the time, TJ was being held at Bridgewater State Hospital, awaiting trial for assault. He had spent most of the summer as a patient in this facility until he was found "competent to stand trial." We were visiting him every other weekend, which was the designated visiting time allocated for patients who were being treated at this facility.

Kayvon had graduated from high school that June. His senior year of high school was eventful, successful, and full of promise. He was the president of the Drama Club, a member of the marching band, and president of the LGBTQ Club. He had been accepted to Parsons School of Design in New York City and would attend their fashion design program. His letters of recommendation from the high school faculty commended him as a young man who was extremely talented in the theater arts and applauded his bravery for being one of the first openly gay students. He was well liked and sociable. Kayvon's passion for fashion design prompted him to design and create gowns for his female friends who were attending their senior prom. The gowns he designed were sought after by his classmates. It was considered a coup to have Kayvon design and create a gown for you.

As a graduation gift, we treated Kayvon to a trip to Spain. He would travel with his sister. They traveled in late August and had a wonderful vacation exploring Barcelona and the surrounding area. I remember visiting TJ at Bridgewater State Hospital while they were away and being careful to not disclose where they were at the time. I felt so badly for TJ. Here he was, being held for an undisclosed amount of time in a facility that was far from desirable, while his sister and brother were gallivanting around Spain. I didn't have the heart to tell him.

We moved Kayvon into his dormitory room at Parsons on Labor Day weekend. It was a whirlwind of activity. Traveling to Manhattan by truck to move him into his Greenwich Village dormitory, meeting his roommate, exploring the campus, and taking a family cruise on the Hudson. We were exhausted, yet excited for Kayvon. He was living his dream. We were excited for him and extremely proud parents.

One month later, the shit hit the fan. It's true that one will always remember exactly what they were doing at the exact moment of a tragedy. For instance, I was in a biology class when I first heard the news of the September 11, 2001 attacks. Most people will tell you they will remember exactly where they were at the time they received the news that the first airplane flew into the Twin Towers.

For me, the same can be said for late September 2007, when less than a month into his freshman year of college, Kayvon called me. I was grocery shopping, standing in the produce aisle by the bananas. Less than two minutes into his call, I began to break into a cold sweat, had goose bumps, my heart started to pound, and a sense of dread overtook me. He wasn't making any sense. He was ranting about a war in the Middle East and afraid that New York City would be bombed. He accused me of hiding information concerning the government. One minute he was screaming angrily, the next minute he sobbed inconsolably. He pleaded with me to come get him and take him home to green grass and trees. He missed nature, bemoaning the "concrete jungle" of New York City. He spoke of Charles Darwin and natural selection. His speech was rapid, his mood labile. Holy Christ, I wondered. Could he be manic, too? Indeed, he was.

I didn't have time to feel sorry for myself or wallow in self-pity. I never do. The way I deal with a situation like this is to promptly take action. How can this new problem be attended to? Who should I call? How do I get prompt and immediate help for my sons?

To start with, I called a close friend of Kayvon's who also was attending college in Manhattan. As soon as I contacted Elizabeth, she sensed the reason for the call. She told me that she was concerned about Kayvon's behavior. He was acting crazy. The previous night, he called her and asked her to meet him at Union Square Park in Greenwich Village. It was a chilly night, yet when she arrived she found Kayvon scantily clad and barefoot. She told me he was skipping around the park and running through the water fountains like a lunatic. Elizabeth began to cry and said she was very worried about him. How could she help?

I needed her to help me get him home. The sooner the better. She told me that she would try to convince him to come home for a couple of days. Take a little break. Get a change of scenery. Thank goodness he agreed. She escorted him to Grand Central Station and tried to get him on the next available bus or train to Boston. It was a nightmare.

Kayvon's mania was escalating rapidly. His erratic behavior resulted in him being escorted off the first two buses that he tried boarding. Elizabeth called me sobbing. She didn't know what to do. Elizabeth was worried that he'd be arrested. She couldn't calm him down. I pleaded with her to keep trying and she finally succeeded. She was able to get him on the third bus and waited and watched as the bus pulled away. Kayvon was on his way home.

The bus ride home must have been tortuous for the other passengers on that bus. Kayvon called us numerous times during the four-hour trip home. He was loud and intrusive one minute, complaining that the person sitting next to him was ignoring him or ecstatically remarking about the wealth of green grass and trees he was passing. He obsessed over Charles Darwin while frantically reading aloud passages from his book on the theory of evolution. It seemed like he grew more unstable as he traveled closer to Boston. His bus finally arrived in Boston, however Kayvon never made it home.

Tom and JoEllen drove into the city to pick Kayvon up from the South Station bus terminal in Boston. JoEllen had been employed for three years at Boston Children's Hospital in its psychiatric unit as a nurse. While working on this unit, she gained experience assisting patients who were suffering with acute mental health issues. She knew Kayvon was most likely displaying symptoms of mania. She called me and told me that they were planning on taking Kayvon to the emergency room of a local hospital to be evaluated instead of driving him home. Tom had other plans.

Five years of experience dealing with TJ's mental health crises had taught us many things. The protocol for someone who is suspected of having a mental health crisis is to take them to the nearest emergency room in a medical hospital for a psychiatric evaluation. We have learned from experience that this is not always the most efficient method of gaining immediate assistance. It takes hours and sometimes days to get someone a bed in a psychiatric facility. As a matter of fact, TJ once waited two days in an emergency room of a Boston hospital while restrained on a stretcher, waiting for a psychiatric admission. It was traumatic and inexcusable.

Tom decided to take matters into his own hands. He and JoEllen drove Kayvon directly to McLean Hospital. They escorted him into the admission building. They informed the guard sitting at the window that Kayvon was manic and should be admitted as he was clearly experiencing a psychiatric emergency. The guard inquired whether they had taken him to a hospital for evaluation. JoEllen requested that a medical professional come and just speak with Kayvon for a few minutes. A psychiatrist working on one of the units in the building met them in the lobby. He interviewed Kayvon for five minutes. Kayvon was admitted immediately with the diagnosis of Bipolar Disorder 1 with psychotic features.

CHAPTER FOURTEEN

Pit Stops

Kayvon would be committed to McLean Hospital for more than two weeks. Upon discharge, he would be required to spend another two weeks in a full day outpatient program, where he would learn coping skills and medication management for his illness. At the time, the most distressing consequence was that he would need to withdraw from college since he had missed too many classes. It would be too difficult to catch up and living in New York City would prove to be far too stressful. Only one month had passed since the day we all made the trip from Massachusetts to New York in a loaded pick-up truck to move Kayvon into his Greenwich Village dorm room. Now, Tom and I needed to make the journey back, just the two of us in an empty truck, to move him out.

We had to obtain permission from the college to retrieve his belongings and had to be escorted to his dorm room once we arrived. When we opened the door to his room, we were shocked. Hundreds of yellow sticky notes with cryptic and nonsensical messages were stuck over every inch of his room on the walls, ceiling, and furniture. We had to precariously step into the room because we couldn't see the floor. Trash, clothing, empty food containers, and debris lined the floor at least a foot deep. I remember standing there in the middle of all the chaos and wondering where to begin. It was a daunting task.

His roommate met us there about an hour after we arrived. I assumed he was curious about Kayvon's whereabouts but I also wondered if he wanted to make certain that we didn't inadvertently confiscate any of his belongings. He told us that he had been worried about Kayvon from the beginning of the semester. Kayvon wasn't sleeping and his erratic behavior was a worry. Living in that small dorm room among all that havoc and turmoil must've been difficult to say the least. While his roommate appeared to be concerned and empathetic, I imagine that it must have been a huge relief to find out that Kayvon would be dropping out of school.

Since his initial diagnosis of bipolar disorder at age 18, Kayvon was accepted to and attended other programs for fashion design. He did go back to Parsons School of Design the following semester but only lasted two months, eventually dropping out after a disciplinary suspension closely followed by his second psychiatric hospitalization. The following year, he attended Fashion Institute of Technology for less than one semester, again failing to complete a semester due to an episode of depression followed by a psychotic break requiring another psychiatric hospitalization. After three failed attempts to attend colleges in New York City, it became evident that Kayvon would need to stay close to home.

Kayvon was able to garner a little more success with college courses while attending colleges closer to home. Living at home and commuting to Boston while attending the School of Fashion Design proved to be more successful for a while. Living at home allowed him to see his local therapist on a regular basis and helped him remain med-compliant. He was able to complete a year of study at this school. Yet, once again, the lack of structure during the summer months led to trouble. That was the summer he ended up spending a month in Cambridge City Jail while awaiting trial for assault and battery.

While Kayvon was incarcerated, I had time to take stock and reflect on the situation at home. It was finally quiet. I was finally able to sleep at night. The tension at home began to dissipate. As much as I knew that Kayvon needed the security of a stable environment, I realized that it was far more important for me to maintain my sanity. Living with Kayvon was toxic. Even on days that I would describe his mood as baseline, neither too manic nor depressed, he is difficult to live with. He's intrusive, loud, erratic, and extremely messy on a good day. He is nasty and inconsiderate on a regular basis. Boundaries are nonexistent, and rules don't apply. I knew he needed to move out, even if it required me to assist in paying for an apartment.

After a one-month incarceration, Kayvon was released from Cambridge City Jail on lesser charges and was served a one-year probation. Incarceration is difficult for everyone. It's meant to be. Being confined to jail is even more difficult for someone with mental illness. Upon his release, it was evident that Kayvon's mental health had decompensated. He would soon require another hospitalization at McLean.

Fortunately, a couple of months later, Kayvon was able to gain admission to Massachusetts College of Art. He procured an apartment in the Mission Hill section in Boston and found a new roommate. It would be a new beginning for Kayvon. He appeared to have finally found his niche and actually flourished at Mass Art. His professors praised his talent, drive, and passion for the extraordinary. His bizarre attire and outlandish mannerisms were considered unique and celebrated within this artistic community. For almost two years, we were finally able to put his mental health problems on the back burner.

Sadly, during this time, his father was diagnosed with Stage Four Squamous Cell Carcinoma, head and neck cancer. We no longer had the time or energy to worry about Kayvon's mental health issues. We had bigger fish to fry. We spent that entire year shuttling back and forth to Boston to seek treatment at the Dana-Farber Cancer Institute. Tom would require chemotherapy and radiation on a weekly or daily basis. Life revolved around cancer treatment and survival.

Once in a while, Kayvon would visit his father at the clinic when he wasn't attending classes. On a few occasions, while visiting the clinic at Dana-Farber, I noticed that Kayvon appeared angry. I assumed the anger was coming from the sadness he may be feeling regarding his father's illness. I never assumed that the anger may be depression caused by his mood disorder. I was too busy and emotionally exhausted to see that my son's symptoms were beginning to spiral out of control. Depression is typically the precursor to mania with Kayvon's bipolar disorder. His mania drove him to believe that placing a backpack on the Boston Marathon finish line on the one-year anniversary of the marathon bombings would be a perfectly executed display of performance art. He didn't see any harm in what he did. He was oblivious.

He was arrested and sent to Bridgewater State Hospital for psychiatric observation. He was suspended from MassArt immediately. This pit stop would be the most profound of all. It has changed his life forever. To this day, he will tell you that he has a difficult time securing employment because of social media. If you Google his name, you'll see that his past mistakes are tattooed on his reputation and may never be eradicated.

It has been four years since the incident at the Boston Marathon finish line. The faculty at MassArt did end up supporting Kayvon, and eventually he was invited back to attend classes. The incident, although not forgiven, was considered to be artistic freedom of speech. In May 2016, Kayvon was able to attend his commencement and walked with his graduating class. However, he had two courses that needed to be completed. He didn't complete them in time. He was hospitalized twice since attending commencement exercises with his graduating class at MassArt in less than one year. However, he has since finished his last two undergraduate courses. It took him 10 years, but he finally earned his degree.

There have been numerous pit stops that Kayvon has encountered since his initial diagnosis of bipolar disorder. He has attended various colleges in the pursuit of completing his undergraduate degree. It's frustrating, expensive, and often daunting. It has taken him 10 years to finally reach that goal. Yet, I have to hand it to him. He has never given up. As a parent of a child with mental illness, you need to accept that there will be a lot of pit stops, speed bumps, and a few fender benders. Goals will take much longer to achieve. But they can be achieved. You simply have to be more patient and accepting. Don't give up.

Discovering that your child will live the remainder of his or her life with a chronic illness is heartbreaking on many levels. It's as if someone has pulled the rug out from under you and knocked you off your feet. You will stumble back up, but never fully recover. You have absolutely no idea the extent of how this illness may affect their life or your own. The promise for a bright and successful future has been diminished. You worry and you grieve for the loss of what could have been. And yes, you feel sorry for yourself. But eventually you accept that burden and allow it to fuel you into becoming the strongest advocate your child will ever have. You become their champion, their spokesperson, and the voice of reason during irrational times. You don't ever give up because you love them.

CHAPTER FIFTEEN

Medical Emergency

While manic shit happens, sleepless nights coupled with the lack of nutrition, and a severe lack of personal hygiene can wreak havoc with one's physical health during a manic episode. TJ, when hypomanic, will ferociously clean himself and his belongings to the point of making his hands raw. However, once his mania becomes full-blown, his showering, washing dishes, and doing laundry becomes secondary or forgotten altogether. To be candid, he stinks. On more than one occasion, TJ's lack of personal hygiene has led to near drastic consequences. During one psychiatric hospitalization, he nearly died.

Psychiatric hospitals treat patients who are mentally ill. The primary objectives for treatment is to keep the patient safe, coupled with evaluation and treatment of the illness with appropriate medication and psychotherapy. Physical health is not considered a primary objective of the treatment plan. Taking care of physical health is secondary to recovery. A medical nurse will be present on the unit to dispense medicine, monitor heart rates and blood pressure, or provide treatment for patients with common illnesses such as diabetes. If a patient contracts a common virus or suffers from a minor headache while hospitalized in a psychiatric setting, he or she may receive suitable treatment or pain management. If the symptoms escalate to the point of becoming dangerous to the patient's physical health, the situation may become life-threatening.

TJ was hospitalized once in mid-December during the holiday season. As with many of his hospitalizations, he was transported by ambulance to the psychiatric facility while on a stretcher in four-point restraints. Due to his large size and past history of assault, he was placed in a private room in order to keep himself, other patients, and the staff safe. Two aides were assigned to his room to make sure he didn't leave and to keep watch over him. In order to calm him down and keep him safe, he would be chemically and physically restrained for days. I was not allowed to visit.

It was frustrating to wait for so long to visit TJ, but I was informed that it was for my own good. I was told by staff that I wouldn't want to see TJ in his current condition. It would be difficult for me to witness and could escalate his erratic behavior. I called the unit and spoke to TJ's psychiatrist and social worker at least three times a day to check on his progress.

After a few days, I was told that TJ had developed symptoms of a virus. He was having difficulty breathing and was coughing a lot. These symptoms were intensifying his agitation. He wasn't eating or drinking fluids. He was becoming more difficult to calm down. They suggested that a visit from me might help to calm TJ down and might help convince him to eat and drink.

When I arrived at the hospital, I was escorted to TJ's "private wing." There were two aides sitting by the door to his room and the door casing was enveloped with towels. I was told that the towels were there to keep the area quiet. TJ was screaming on a regular basis and any outside noise was causing him to become unsettled. They asked me to enter the room as quietly as possible so I wouldn't disturb him if he were sleeping.

When I entered the room, I noticed that a third person was sitting on a chair in the corner of TJ's room, keeping watch. The room was dark with no windows or furniture except the bed and two chairs. I pulled a chair up beside TJ's bed. I could hear TJ's labored breathing and see how pale his coloring was. His lips were chapped and his mouth was crusted over with dried saliva. His coloring was off. I held his hand and whispered to him that I was there. He slowly opened one eye and tried to focus on me. He began to cry and moan painfully. It was pathetic. When he tried to talk, I could hear the phlegm in his throat making his speech garbled. I pleaded with him to try to drink something and held a glass of water with a straw to his lips. He was so congested, he couldn't get the liquid down. I became very concerned.

Something was not adding up. While chemically restrained, TJ typically slurs his speech, sleeps fitfully, and can barely walk. But, this was entirely different. I was very concerned because he wasn't eating or drinking. He was clearly struggling to breathe. I asked the aide sitting in the room if a nurse had been by to check on him. Had anyone taken his temperature or listened to his lungs? A nurse was soon called into TJ's room to check his vitals. Within the hour, TJ was transported by ambulance to the closest medical facility. He had pneumonia.

If a psychiatric patient has to leave the facility to receive emergency treatment at a medical facility, he is escorted by ambulance in physical restraints. Once admitted for treatment, he or she will be placed in a private room and monitored 24 hours a day by security. As soon as the patient recovers from the medical emergency, he'll be transported back to the psychiatric facility in the same manner. Within a week, TJ returned. His health had improved significantly and his mania was subsiding. He was soon allowed to roam the unit with the patient population, attend group therapy meetings, and meet with his social workers and psychotherapists. I often wonder if the lack of medical treatment he received at the onset of pneumonia had prolonged his recovery to mental health.

A few years later, a more serious medical emergency occurred while TJ was manic. This incident was far more severe and could have led to dire consequences. One evening, I received a phone call from TJ's landlord. She told me that she confronted him to turn the volume down on his music which was blaring at all hours of the night. She called me not to complain, but because she was concerned. She said that his apartment was a mess, he appeared disheveled, and that he seemed to be struggling mentally.

I try to stay in contact with my boys on a regular basis. I text or call them several times weekly. I can often tell their mental state by the sound of their voice or the nature of their texts. When Kayvon is not mentally stable, he becomes persistent in making monetary demands. TJ becomes argumentative and angry. I had not spoken with TJ for a few days but sensed that he wasn't doing well mentally. What surprised me when his landlord called was that she also expressed concern regarding TJ's physical health. His landlord also was a nurse. She told me that TJ had a wound on his leg that appeared alarming. His entire leg was red and swollen. The wound would need to be treated as soon as possible. She knew he needed psychiatric help, but the wound on his leg was serious and required immediate attention. She had a plan.

She told me that she was going back downstairs to TJ's apartment to convince him to go to the hospital to have his leg examined. To this day, I'm not sure how she pulled this scheme off but she also convinced him that he should call for an ambulance. When the ambulance arrived, she spoke to the EMTs who would transport TJ to the closest medical hospital and told them he also would need a psychiatric evaluation. She pulled the scheme off!

TJ was admitted to the hospital with a MRSA infection in his leg. It was a serious type of staph infection that required intravenous antibiotics to treat. If it wasn't treated immediately, the end result would have resulted in amputation. His psychiatric evaluation concluded that he also was manic and psychotic. He would receive treatment for the MRSA infection as well as psychiatric treatment for his bipolar disorder in the medical unit of the hospital. Two armed security guards would keep watch outside his door.

As soon as TJ's infection responded to the antibiotics and he was beginning to recover medically, he was admitted to the psychiatric floor of the hospital. He would continue to receive oral antibiotics to treat the MRSA infection and medical personnel would visit him on the psychiatric unit to monitor his progress. No one anticipated how dangerous the situation would become.

Within a week, TJ's mental and physical health declined dramatically. He became disoriented and delusional. It was assumed that his mania and psychosis had worsened, so dosage increases to his psychiatric medications were prescribed. As the medication dosages increased, his confusion got substantially worse. He stopped eating and drinking. He became frantic. He was placed in a "quiet room" with padded walls and no windows, containing a small cot without sheets for his safety.

I called to check on TJ several times each day. Once again, I was advised not to visit as TJ's condition may frighten or sadden me. I was told that his mania and psychosis were being controlled, but he was having a difficult time.

Finally, after a few days the hospital called and asked me to come in. Once again, they considered that it might help to calm TJ down if he saw me. I'll never forget what I saw. As I walked into the unit, I could hear a noise that sounded like a wild animal keening. While I was being escorted through the unit, I soon discovered that horrible sound was coming from the "quiet room" that contained my son.

TJ was partially covered with a hospital johnny. He was lying on the cot and writhing restlessly. A male aide was trying to get TJ to eat or drink. TJ couldn't sit up. His speech was barely coherent. He was crying one minute and moaning the next. It was pitiful to see. TJ's sobbing intensified once he recognized that I was present in the room. He began yelling to me but his voice was so muddled I couldn't comprehend what he was trying to say. From the cot he reached up to me, hugging me, and repeated what he was trying to say. I then realized he was pleading, "Help me."

I became frantic. What the hell was happening to my son? Within minutes, the psychiatric nurse and other medical attendants entered the room. I told them that there was something seriously wrong with TJ and that his condition needed to be addressed immediately. I explained that I have seen him at his worst, but his present state was far more extreme than I had ever witnessed. They called for immediate and urgent assistance from medical units in the hospital.

TJ was in the midst of renal failure. They found that his creatinine level was dangerously high. His kidneys were failing. There was functional damage to his kidneys due to his MRSA infection and resulting dehydration. TJ was demonstrating all the classic symptoms of increased creatinine levels: confusion, weakness, fatigue, and dehydration. However, his symptoms were confused with symptoms of a person who was taking high doses of antipsychotics and mood stabilizers. If I hadn't come to visit TJ that evening, he may have gone into complete renal failure.

TJ's recovery was slow, yet steady. He remained in the psychiatric unit of the hospital but was treated medically on a regular basis until he totally regained kidney function. It took two weeks for him to walk on his own. The most frightening feature that TJ displayed was confusion. I remember bringing letters and cards that family members had written and giving them to TJ to read. For a while, he could barely open the envelopes, as if he couldn't get his hands to work. He had difficulty reading the cards and would get frustrated and throw them against the wall. It was heartbreaking. A team of doctors treating TJ told me that they couldn't guarantee that he would regain full function. Eventually he did recover both mentally and physically. It took time, but after six weeks, he walked out of that psychiatric unit on his own, healthy and strong.

While TJ was hospitalized during that particular episode, a social worker asked me a question I will never forget. He wondered why I was reluctant to place TJ in a group home instead of allowing him to live on his own. I remember his exact words: "Why can't you accept that TJ isn't capable of living on his own?" I remember feeling violated. That's the only way to describe how I felt. In my heart at that instant, despite the fact that he had been hospitalized more than 25 times in 10 years, I knew that TJ was very capable. I remember telling that social worker that I knew my son better than he did. I saw TJ as competent, intelligent, and extremely capable of living on his own. He didn't need to live in a group home. He just needed time to accept his illness and recovery.

It has been more than three years since TJ has been hospitalized. He completed his undergraduate degree, graduating from the University of Massachusetts Boston, and is working part time. He takes his medications religiously, sees his therapist on a regular basis, and is maintaining his sobriety. He has accomplished all of this while living alone.

My recommendation is to trust your instincts. If you're raising a child or living with someone you love who is suffering from mental illness, you must remain vigilant. You know them better than anyone else. You see them during the times when they're doing well and also during the times when they're suffering. If you think something is not right, even in a medical setting while being treated by medical professionals, speak out. You are truly their best advocate. To this day, TJ will tell everyone that I have saved his life. I suppose, in a manner of speaking, I have. But, he has, too.

CHAPTER SIXTEEN

There's No Place Like Home, Hospitals,
and Mental Health Facilities

As I'm writing this book, I can honestly say that TJ is doing the best he ever has done since his initial diagnosis at age 17. He is currently 32. His 15-year journey toward recovery has been arduous to say the least. He has had to live in various mental health facilities, each stay mandated by either the Department of Mental Health or the Commonwealth of Massachusetts. Some of these places were high-security, state-run locked buildings and other places allowed TJ the freedom to come and go at his will. They have all proven to be an integral purpose toward TJ's road to recovery.

TJ has not lived under my roof since the age of 20. At age 20, he was committed to Bridgewater State Hospital for two months. For the first few days of that commitment, TJ was locked in a tiny cell in solitary confinement, containing only a metal cot. He was intoxicated when he was admitted to Bridgewater State Hospital, and spent those initial days tortuously withdrawing from crack cocaine and other opiates. The only item of clothing he was allowed to wear was a plastic poncho. The cot he laid on was void of a mattress, sheets, and blankets. If he vomited, urinated, or defecated, he was hosed down. I know this because he remembers. I also know this because I called the staff on his unit at least three times a day to check on him. It was difficult at first to get in touch with someone on TJ's unit in order to get information about him. One has to diligently navigate the various voice prompts at most state-run facilities in order to finally speak to a live human being. It's frustrating and takes patience, but it's worth the effort. When I finally connected with a nurse on TJ's unit, I was relieved. I remember the first thing she said to me: "Good for you. You're his mom? I'm glad you called. You can't imagine how seldom people call to check up on patients who are staying here. We have no idea what your son is like when he is doing well. It helps us to get a better picture of who he really is. It's important for us to know that there are people on the outside who truly care about their care and comfort." For the next few weeks, until the time TJ was able to have visitors, she became my ally, TJ's advocate, and my only connection to my son. To this day, I consider that nurse to be an angel.

Once TJ was deemed well enough to leave that unit, he was placed in another locked unit at Bridgewater State Hospital with the general population. He also was finally allowed to have visitors. We were only allowed to visit every other weekend and for a limited time frame. Everything in our life was put on hold in order to meet those particular times that we could visit TJ. He counted the days until we came. We became his lifeline and we couldn't let him down.

The drive to Bridgewater took an hour. If visiting hours began at 2 p.m., we would leave our house at noon in order to allow time for travel and to fill out all the necessary paperwork required to see him. Once we arrived, locked our personal belongings in a locker, and filled out visitor paperwork, we had to stand in line to be admitted into the visitor area. Once we finally made it to the security guard who checked our paperwork and our photo identification, TJ's unit was notified that he had visitors. Then, we had to clear the metal detectors and body checks to enter the waiting room. This all took a considerable amount of time. If the line to check in was long or slow, our visit would be shortened. Visiting hours ended promptly at 4 p.m. Often, we didn't even make it into the visitor area until 3:00 p.m., despite the fact that we arrived an hour early. One time, after the one-hour drive and lengthy check-in process, 15 minutes were all that remained for our visit.

When we finally entered the locked visitor lounge, we had to wait for TJ to arrive. He sometimes arrived alone or escorted by one guard. Other times, he arrived in a lineup along with other patients/inmates from his unit. Imagine seeing your 19-year-old son shackled with chains at the ankles and wrists while wearing an orange jump suit, bearing the Department of Corrections logo. I had to catch my breath and hold back tears in order to appear happy to see him. This was not a room where crying was appropriate.

The room was crowded and loud. We were surrounded by wives, children, mothers, fathers, and friends of the other patients/inmates. A security station was located at the front of the room and manned by several guards who kept close watch over the population. They were looking for any type of suspicious behavior and extraneous displays of affection. A warning would be issued if a visitor hugged or kissed an inmate for an extended amount of time. Private conversations were impossible.

The main attraction located in the visitor lounge was the vending machines. Visitors could purchase vending machine debit cards in the check-in area in order to purchase snacks or candy in the visitor's lounge. To this day, I'm not sure if TJ was happier to see us or to purchase snacks from the vending machines. Access to the vending machines was certainly the highlight of his and most other inmates' visits.

Often, during the visit, a loud alarm would sound. It was frightening and ominous. When the alarm sounded, the guards would order the inmates to "line up against the wall." It was called a "count." It occurred several times a day and was a way of keeping track of the population who are currently housed inside the facility. The count often lasted several minutes, and no talking was allowed. I recall on one visit that the count was off. As a result, all the inmates were marched back to their units, and visiting hours abruptly ended.

Can you even imagine being mentally ill, suffering from psychosis, mania, or depression and having to survive in an atmosphere such as this? The patients, who are actually treated like prison inmates, are herded like cattle to visit with their loved ones. The food is horrific, lacking in nutrition and hardly palatable. Patients, like my son at the time, may be simply awaiting trial for a crime they have not even been found guilty of, yet they're treated like a criminal. Physical contact from loved ones is prohibited during visits. Many of them are not allowed outside for fresh air or sunshine. An insignificant amount of psychotherapy or behavioral therapy is available on a regular basis. The only source of regular treatment is medication. It is ludicrous to think that this is a suitable or recuperative atmosphere for treatment.

TJ, at age 19, was considered to be an adult in the eyes of the law. Because he was no longer considered a juvenile, he was placed in the adult facility Bridgewater State Hospital, where he was probably one of the youngest patients spending time there. The patient population in his unit were all mentally ill and were either being held there while awaiting trial or committed there for crimes for which they already were found guilty. TJ's fellow patients included rapists, child molesters, and murderers. There were gang members present. After a visit from his sister, JoEllen, a fellow patient offered TJ immunity from his gang if TJ could promise him a date with her upon his release. (TJ didn't accept the offer.) TJ has told me he witnessed many disturbing things while at Bridgewater but would never fully disclose to me what he saw. It is too difficult to talk about.

The thing that amazes me is that as horrific and unsettling as this experience was for TJ, he will tell you it was the time he spent at Bridgewater that was what ultimately led him to sobriety. Any recovering alcoholic, drug addict, or substance abuser will tell you that they had to eventually hit rock bottom in order to finally accept that they were an addict and seek help. While at Bridgewater, after detoxing in his solitary cell, a fellow patient told TJ that he would end up spending his life locked up in places like this or die if he didn't change his ways. Since that day, TJ has remained sober. He began attending Alcoholics Anonymous meetings on a regular basis while in Bridgewater and still does to this day. In a manner of speaking, the time spent at Bridgewater did help TJ heal from one aspect of his mental illness, his substance abuse.

After two months, TJ was transported from Bridgewater to Taunton State Hospital. After his two-month stay at Bridgewater, he was still considered to be incompetent to stand trial and would remain in Taunton for six months in order to receive further treatment. Taunton State Hospital is not a pretty place. Far from it. The ancient and decrepit buildings located on the hospital grounds appear gloomy and somewhat foreboding. Many of the dark and vacant buildings are overgrown with ivy and shattered windows, adding to the formidable and somber atmosphere. One rarely sees anyone walking on the hundreds of acres. Frankly, the hospital grounds and its surrounding buildings would be the perfect place to stage a horror movie.

Taunton State Hospital is a locked, psychiatric, state-run facility that is highly secure but offers a little more freedom than the Bridgewater facility. Visiting hours are far less restrictive than at Bridgewater, and visitors are allowed on the patient's unit to visit. Security is stringent but far less rigorous as when one pays a visit to Bridgewater. When we entered Taunton State Hospital to visit TJ, we had to lock our purses and coats in a locker and were personally escorted onto the unit. There were no metal detectors, body searches, or dress codes. After a certain amount of time, when it was deemed safe to do so and while supervised, patients were allowed off the unit to have their meals at a separate cafeteria in another building on the grounds. This was considered to be a significant reward given to patients who exhibited appropriate behavior. Taunton also offers some therapeutic groups, one-on-one counseling, and psychotherapy to its patients. I suppose one could definitely consider Taunton to be a step up from Bridgewater, but a state hospital is still a far cry from the mental health services offered from a private hospital such as McLean Hospital.

The thing that was most disheartening to me was the length of time that many patients remained at this facility. Some are housed at this type of state-run facility for months or years while awaiting trial or when found "guilty by reason of insanity" and committed there. Many patients are found to be too dangerous to be placed in a residential home or released to live among the general population. Often, when a patient is finally considered to be mentally stable and dismissed from criminal charges, the process of securing housing is what often holds up their release. Finding appropriate housing is a lengthy and laborious process.

The six months spent at Taunton State Hospital proved to be valuable to TJ's mental health for a variety of reasons. He continued to remain sober and with sobriety his medications became more and more effective as the months wore on. His fun-loving and charismatic personality began to re-emerge. He began to draw and paint again. The combination of sobriety, medication compliancy, and psychotherapy cleared his mind. He finally seemed to get it. He grew to accept the fact that he couldn't drink alcohol or abuse drugs and needed to stay on his medications if he wanted to live a better life. The staff grew to appreciate TJ's quick wit and creativity and soon noticed that he was improving dramatically. They began offering him more privileges and freedom. After three months, he was allowed to come home to visit for 24 hours. A month later, he earned a pass to leave for the entire weekend.

I remember being happy that TJ was coming home to visit. It would be nice to spend the entire weekend with him instead of short visits on a crowded psychiatric unit. Yet, I also recall the tremendous feeling of anxiety these visits caused me. It was a huge responsibility and scary step for us. Will TJ want to go out with his old friends? Will he remain sober? Will he try to escape our watch and lose all that he had gained? Will he remember to take his medications? We worried that we weren't capable of handling him.

We sensed that TJ also was nervous about how he'd handle all this newfound freedom. He had just spent nearly five months living in lockdown under 24-hour supervision, being told what to do and when to do it. At the beginning, he was like a fish out of water. He seemed like a lost soul. He just wanted to spend time with us and did not even try to contact his old friends. We hid all the alcohol in the house before his visit, just in case he would try to sneak a drink. But, this was not an issue. Once TJ settled in at home, he was content to spend time with us. Fortunately, the visits went relatively smoothly.

Taunton had developed a system in order to prevent many of these issues from potentially happening. While on his 24 or 48-hour pass, TJ had to contact someone on his unit a few times a day to check in. He was given specific times to take his medications and was told to call the nurse on his unit as soon as he took them. His visits were for specific amount of times (24-48 hours) and he had a curfew to get back to the hospital within that time frame. Upon his arrival, the hospital administered drug and alcohol tests. TJ never faltered, proving to the staff and the Department of Mental Health that he had developed the tools needed to move on. He was ready to take the next step to recovery. His next placement would be a group home, run by the Department of Mental Health as soon as a suitable arrangement was secured. TJ was pleased when he received the notification that a bed became available in a residential group home called the Reading House. This would be TJ's home for the next year.

Once TJ was transferred to the Reading House, our lives became a little more manageable. This group home is located only two miles from us. Scheduling visits with TJ during his stay at Bridgewater or Taunton State Hospital was an all-consuming event as each of those facilities were located at least an hour away. Visits to TJ at the Reading House were less restrictive and far more pleasant.

Reading House is a group home operated by the Massachusetts Department of Mental Health. TJ lived there with five other residents, all adult men with various mental health diagnoses. Each resident had their own bedroom, but shared common space such as the living room, bathrooms, and kitchen/dining room. TJ was allowed to bring items from home for his bedroom in order to make him more comfortable. It was a bright and pleasant house located in Reading, MA.

The Reading House is operated by staff who are employed by the Department of Mental Health to administer medication, transport the residents, and offer onsite counseling. Residents are encouraged to leave the house during the daytime hours after breakfast and before dinner. Some of the residents had small jobs and others attended partial outpatient day programs run by local mental health community outreach programs. Residents also are encouraged to attend Alcoholics Anonymous meetings in the local area. TJ attended a partial day program for the first month of his stay and went to an AA meeting at least once or twice weekly.

The goal of the group home is to smoothly transition its residents into independent living while living in a safe environment. The residents share all the common household chores necessary to keep the home running smoothly. They shop for groceries, cook, help to maintain the shared space, keep their private bedrooms neat, and take care of the trash. There are rules such as evening curfews and random substance abuse testing. Each resident is assigned a social worker or liaison from the Department of Mental Health who oversees their counseling, psychiatric appointments, and benefits from Social Security, such as disability income or food stamps.

Living at the Reading House was possibly the most valuable experience for TJ. Living there provided him the tools required to someday live independently. After his first month, TJ was admitted into a day program offered by Boston University called the Center for Psychiatric Rehabilitation. Entrance into this program was limited, but his DMH liaison encouraged him to apply. It is a noncredit recovery education program offered on the Boston University campus and run by the psychology department. Students are allowed to choose a variety of wellness courses. The courses that are offered help to further develop tools needed for rehabilitation and recovery, such as stress management, meditation, yoga, exercise, art, music and film. While attending courses there, the students are observed by staff and students who are majoring in psychology, psychiatry, or counseling. It's a win-win situation for all. Another advantage for TJ was that he had to learn to navigate public transportation into Boston each day he attended the program. He was growing more independent with each day.

TJ did experience a setback while living at Reading House. Medication management can be extremely complex especially when prescribing certain mood stabilizers such as lithium. Lithium levels have to be monitored on a regular basis to ensure the medication is operating at a therapeutic level. Weight gain or loss can dramatically affect the efficacy of lithium. Many psychiatrists are reluctant to keep their patients on high levels of lithium for long durations since the drug can cause tremors, weight gain, and thirst. Lithium, when used for a long period of times, also can result in liver damage. For all these reasons, TJ's psychiatrist would try to offer alternative, safer mood stabilizers to replace or reduce the amount of lithium that was prescribed. It didn't work. As TJ's lithium levels reduced, even while on alternative mood stabilizers and while maintaining his sobriety, TJ became manic.

As his lithium levels diminished, his mania developed quickly and without much warning. TJ became psychotic and paranoid seemingly overnight, and the staff at the Reading House called an ambulance and had him transported to a local psychiatric hospital. Luckily, he was stabilized relatively quickly and returned to Reading House within weeks. Since then, TJ has remained on lithium. He has his levels checked on a regular basis and is diligent about taking this medication. Lithium may not be the best medication for the long term, but it seems to be the only mood stabilizer that has worked for

TJ. Sometimes, you have to choose your battles. Despite all of its negative side effects, Lithium has been TJ's wonder drug.

After TJ underwent months of rehabilitation and stability while living at Reading House, it became apparent to the staff, his DMH liaisons, and to TJ that he was ready for the next step. He was prepared to live independently, albeit with assistance from services offered from the Department of Mental Health. His name had been placed on a list for Section 8 housing and he would receive a voucher to live in an apartment subsidized by the state based on his Social Security Disability Income. We were going apartment hunting!

Based on his disability income, TJ was given a price range of what he could afford for housing. His DMH liaison suggested a metropolitan area located on the MBTA bus and subway system route since he relied on public transportation. He did his research and chose to live in Malden, a city located close to Boston, yet far enough away to be affordable, offering several apartments close to public transportation. After a few weeks of searching, TJ found the ideal apartment located in a large two-family home on a quiet street within walking distance to the bus and subway lines. It was the perfect fit.

I will never forget how we both fell instantly in love with this apartment as soon as we walked in. The rooms were sunny and spacious, consisting of lots of windows and wood floors. It offered ample room for TJ's musical instruments and artwork. And it would be available within a week!

The landlord, a wonderful woman who owned the home and lived upstairs with her family, turned out to be a blessing to TJ. She seemed to immediately sense that TJ was not the typical tenant. When we viewed the apartment, TJ and I were accompanied by his DMH liaison. I remember seeing the landlord quietly speaking to his liaison in the kitchen while TJ and I were looking at the bedroom. As it turns out, TJ's DMH liaison disclosed that TJ was a client in the mental health system assuring her that rent would be paid through the state on a regular basis. The landlord never hesitated. She instantly informed TJ that he was welcome to rent her apartment. A few months later, once TJ was settled, the landlord told me that she had someone in her family living with mental illness. She understood the challenges TJ faced and was happy she could offer TJ a safe place to live.

Before TJ moved into his apartment, the Mission of Deeds, a nonprofit volunteer organization that provides beds, used furniture, and household items to people in need, offered assistance and allowed TJ to shop their local thrift store for donated furniture and kitchen items. A social worker, employed by the local community outreach program operated by the Department of Mental Health, came by the apartment to check on TJ at least once a week. A nurse visited TJ each morning to administer his medication. He was able to live independently because of all the services that were set up for him through the Department of Mental Health. This apartment has been home to TJ for more than eight years. It has been his safe haven.

Looking back, I realize the importance of every step that TJ had to take in order to live somewhat independently. Bridgewater State Hospital, as horrible as it was, allowed TJ to realize his need to embrace sobriety. Taunton State Hospital, although a locked and secure facility, accommodated more freedom for visits and far more mental health services than Bridgewater. However, had TJ been released from Bridgewater and sent home, it probably would have resulted in failure. He needed the structure and limits that Taunton offered. He needed to be in a place that ensured his continued sobriety. Walking out of Bridgewater a free man would've been like stepping off a cliff. TJ would've faltered and fallen hard. The year spent at Reading House provided TJ with the services and mechanisms he needed to live more independently. By the time TJ moved into his apartment, he was armed with all that he needed to succeed.

I wish I could say that life was like a bowl of cherries once TJ moved into his apartment. That hasn't always been the case. That's probably never going to be the case. However, life has been better for TJ. Medication adjustments or stress from changes in TJ's life have led to manic or psychotic episodes often resulting in hospitalization. Fortunately, for the past 10 years, TJ has been under the auspices of the Department of Mental Health and his mental health crises have been dealt with relatively quickly. The last time TJ was hospitalized was when he was admitted with the MRSA infection in his leg. That was more than three years ago. Since then, TJ has lived independently because he does what he needs to do in order to stay mentally well.

CHAPTER SEVENTEEN

The Light at the end of the Tunnel

I can see it now. It has been a long dark journey, but I can now see a glimmer of hope shining off in the distance. The light seems to be growing stronger and brighter with each passing year. That's the key. Time, persistence, and maturity have brought enlightenment.

Fifteen years ago, I sat in a support group meeting led by NAMI, the National Association for Mental Illness. The meeting was held at McLean Hospital and addressed issues common to parents of children with mental illness. I attended this meeting about one year after TJ's initial diagnosis. I sat in a large circle along with a group of parents who were raising children, varying from ages 17–50 with mental illness. The stories were all similar, many were depressing or painfully heartbreaking. Stories of adults who had lost their jobs and their homes, destroyed their marriages, had been arrested, or were now homeless. The most valuable piece of advice I garnered from that evening, the one statement that gave me hope, was spoken by the group facilitator who was also a parent of a young adult with mental illness. He said that age brought wisdom. Sometimes, all it takes is the maturity that comes with age in order for someone to accept their mental illness. You just have to be patient.

I want to be clear about this. Don't be misled. With age comes acceptance. That doesn't mean that a person will outgrow the illness. They don't ever outgrow the illness, they learn how to grow along with the illness. Eventually, they learn to manage their medication, deal with the stressors that often exasperate the mood disorder and continue to attend counseling on a regular basis.

In the early years, our hopes and dreams that our sons would someday live a productive and happy life were often filled with doubt. Frankly, there were many days that I thought one of them would die from a drug overdose or kill themselves. When TJ lived at home, there were several mornings that I would enter TJ's bedroom to wake him up and would hold my breath, wondering if I'd find him alive. Living with uncertainty and chaos became a way of life.

Yet, during those tumultuous years at the beginning of my son's diagnoses, I had to figure out ways to help them cope until they reached a point in their lives when it would finally click. Since their initial diagnosis at age 17 for TJ and age 19 for Kayvon, that day would be a long time coming. Many times we wondered if they'd ever get it. TJ has finally accepted his illness and is working on establishing a life for himself while managing his symptoms. For him, maturity has brought wisdom. On the other hand, there are many days that I still wonder if Kayvon will ever get it. He is now 29 years old. He has accepted that he has Bipolar Disorder but is reluctant to do what is necessary in order to lead a productive life. He struggles to adapt and comply with the norms of society. He is a square peg trying to fit into a round hole. His Bipolar Disorder is being managed but his underlying personality disorder complicates everything. Maybe, Kayvon will get it someday. Maybe not.

So how do I survive day to day? How do I maintain my sanity throughout all of these years of insanity? I never give up. During the worst of times, when one or both sons are experiencing psychosis and mania, I simply keep my head above water and wade through all the crap and find my way to safety. It takes persistence, patience, and strength. I must be stronger than the illness in order to survive because they rely on my strength for survival.

The journey has not ended. It never will. But, now I can say, "I've been there. I've done that. I can deal with that." During those 15 years while my sons were gaining maturity and learning to accept their illness, I was discovering ways to help. I've managed to navigate the mental health system, cultivated the means for securing services that my sons needed, and learned the importance of caring for myself.

CHAPTER EIGHTEEN

911

Getting help for someone during a psychiatric emergency is not easy. Far from it. It's never as simple as scheduling a sick appointment with your primary care physician or walking into an urgent care clinic for immediate assistance. Psychiatrists and therapists are few and far between and finding one who will take a new patient can take weeks or months. It's frustrating, tricky, and not practical if the situation is of an urgent nature. So how do you begin?

For me, it began at the emergency room at a local hospital almost 15 years ago. TJ was 17 years old, high on drugs and alcohol, and displaying full-blown mania. He was out of control and combative. Early that evening, TJ assaulted our neighbor while he was trying to restrain TJ in order to calm him down. That was the first time TJ was involuntarily admitted to a psychiatric facility. The Commonwealth of Massachusetts issued a "72-hour hold" because he was found to be a threat to himself or someone else. He was "pink-slipped." It wouldn't be his last time.

I don't know if other states have laws similar to Massachusetts when it comes to issuing an emergency 72-hour hold to someone in an emergent and dangerous psychiatric state. I can't vouch for other states or countries but can tell you that the Massachusetts ordinance has saved TJ numerous times. TJ has never willfully admitted himself for psychiatric care. He fights it tooth and nail. He has barricaded himself in his room, ran away from help when we've called the police for assistance, jumped out of moving vehicles when we were on our way to the hospital, and lied about his identity when approached by police. In other words, he has been a threat to himself.

He also has tried to cause harm to others while psychotic or manic. TJ's mania would cause TJ to become aggressive and out of control. The thoughts in his head would become so loud that he'd do anything to try to quiet his restless mind, he would drink, use drugs, play his music deafeningly loud, throw things, break things, bang his head against a wall. I imagine it must be torture for TJ, but it was also tortuous to live with.

One summer day, I was sitting in my backyard with my sister. She knew TJ was having a manic episode and came to see if she could help me convince him to go to the hospital. As we sat there, we watched as TJ threw items out of his bedroom window smashing them to the ground below. One by one, he frenetically tossed CDs, sports trophies, glass-framed awards he received in middle and high school, his high school yearbook, and ceramic art work he had created out the window. The music coming from his bedroom was intrusive and ear splitting. While we witnessed the frenzy and chaos, I began to worry that he would jump out of the window himself.

His father came home and tried to stop the ensuing disaster. He pleaded with him to calm down and begged TJ to allow him to take him to a hospital for help. TJ began throwing things at his father. We called for police intervention when TJ just missed hitting his father in the head with telephone. By the time the police arrived, TJ and his father were going after one another with golf clubs. When the police stormed into the house, TJ took off, running down the street. He was caught within the hour, arrested for attempted assault, and brought to the local jail. The local crisis team was called and he was again "pink-slipped" and brought to the closest psychiatric facility. TJ was deemed a threat to himself and others and held for observation for 72 hours.

So what happens once the 72 hours are up? Technically, in the state of Massachusetts, once the 72-hour commitment is complete, the patient has the legal right to walk out of the hospital. Luckily, there are loopholes or safety measures in place that can prevent this from happening if the patient isn't ready to be discharged. All the psychiatric facilities at which TJ or Kayvon have been treated, employ lawyers who represent the patient as well as the hospital. These lawyers are called in to the hospital to advocate for the patient's safety. They interview the patient to determine whether further hospitalization is required. If, after the interview and review of hospital notes, the lawyer feels that the patient is not able to make a competent decision regarding their care, they advocate to the court for additional time. This process can go on and on.

Thankfully, once the mania and psychosis has subsided, both of my sons agree to stay in the hospital until they are completely ready for discharge. Once their minds have quieted, their judgment is less impaired. I am very thankful that the 72-hour hold exists. It's just unfortunate that it has to exist. That's the nature of mental illness. Nothing is easy.

During the course of 15 or more years, I've dealt with this type of emergency at least 40 times. There was a point in my life that my sons were brought to the hospital by police cruisers or ambulances so often that whenever I saw an ambulance approaching my neighborhood I panicked.

I recently met with a friend who had just called to have her son taken by ambulance due to a psychiatric emergency. She was an emotional mess and needed to talk to someone who understood what it was like to raise a son with mental illness. She was embarrassed. She told me it was humiliating to have to call the police to get help for her son and worried what the neighbors would think. I told her to let it go. She was doing the right thing. It's so unfortunate that there is this enormous stigma attached to mental illness. If a neighbor called an ambulance for a medical emergency such as a heart attack or automobile accident, no one would hide behind the curtains and judge. Calling 911 is the only way to get help as efficiently as possible for a psychiatric emergency, too. And when your child or loved one is having an emergency, who cares what others think?

CHAPTER NINETEEN

Navigating the System

Some people may call me sneaky. Others may call me resourceful. I prefer the latter. When it comes to navigating the mental health system, I have become somewhat of an expert at going over and under the many loopholes it contains. I have had to. In order to gain information and advocate for my sons, I have had to discover ways of getting around HIPAA (Health Insurance Portability and Accountability Act of 1996) laws, hospital policies, and my sons' demands for privacy while they are clearly not of sound mind. Negotiating the phone systems, staff, and sometimes fellow patients during the course of at least 40 hospitalizations have taught me to be sly like a fox. The fox always gets its prey.

Imagine your child or spouse has finally been picked up by an ambulance because he or she is in the middle of a psychiatric emergency. You have endured the living hell of dealing with them while their mania or psychosis has been escalating to the point of being emergent. They haven't eaten or slept for days. They've been loud, threatening, and argumentative. You have been pleading with them to no avail to take their medication, see their therapist, or seek help at a psychiatric facility. They refuse to seek help because they are being fueled by that glorious and enticing euphoria that accompanies mania. Basically, you're waiting until they get sick enough to call an ambulance or the police or walking on eggshells until they get to the point when they threaten to physically harm you or harm themselves.

TJ's mania and psychosis once became so alarming that it affected him physically. On this occasion, he became so psychotic that he believed he was Jesus Christ. During this manic episode, he displayed physical symptoms that were outrageous and disturbing. He sat in his bedroom chanting gibberish for hours and actually urinated on his rug. He referred to himself as the new Christ. Over the course of a few hours, his body began to stiffen to the point that he couldn't walk or sit. He had difficulty blinking. I remember the feeling of distress and helplessness I felt. The look of panic on TJ's face was disconcerting. I didn't know what to do or where to turn. I called his psychiatrist and he asked to speak to TJ. He proposed that TJ was experiencing a neurological condition called Dystonia, a muscle disorder caused by faulty brain signals. They suggested that he may also be having a panic attack. His psychiatrist told him to take Benadryl to help him calm down until he got to the closest emergency room. This episode was different from any other manic or psychotic episode because this time, TJ agreed to have us take him to be treated. He was scared.

It may be difficult to imagine the all-encompassing feeling of relief that occurs while your loved one is being taken away from you against their will or they're admitted for hospitalization because they are considered a harm to his or herself. If you've ever lived through the uncertainty and helplessness of dealing with someone else's craziness you can empathize. The house is finally quiet. You can finally breathe. Someone else is dealing with their problems. It's out of your hands. You can go home, pick up the pieces, and wait while they get the professional help they desperately need.

By the next day, once peace and sanity has been restored to my home, I am mentally and physically prepared for an update. I want to know where my son is, whether he has been admitted to a psychiatric facility, and what his current health status is. I want answers and I want them ASAP. Unfortunately, no one will tell me anything. The road blocks begin to build up. I'm told that my son is over the age of 17 and considered an adult. I am not allowed to gain any information because he hasn't signed the release that allows me to receive information. The frustration and tension begins to mount again. I'm no longer dealing with my son's mania, I'm dealing with the system.

My first step is to call the emergency room located in the hospital where my son was evaluated. I simply call the hospital's main phone number and ask to be connected to the emergency room. Then I give the ER my son's name and ask whether he is still being treated in the ER. Typically, someone answering the phone will answer yes or no. If the answer is no, the next step is to find out where they were transported to. If I'm lucky, I am told the name of the psychiatric facility he was transported to by ambulance. But that's not always the case.

Typically, I'm informed that my son was no longer in the ER and transported to another facility. However, due to privacy laws, they are not able to provide me with any more information. That's when I move to the next step. I call the ambulance company that services that particular hospital. Once I call and give them my son's name, asking when and where this company has transported my son, I'm usually provided with a time and a location. Once I find out where my son is being treated, I take the next step and call that hospital.

In most cases, when I call the main phone number of the psychiatric hospital and ask which unit he is being treated on, they simply connect me to that unit. Bingo! I know where he is and that he's getting help. Yet, obtaining more specific information about my son's condition is always the most difficult step. Typically, a nurse or social worker working on this particular unit will tell me they can't give me any information about my son since he hasn't signed a release to provide me with details concerning his care. I don't get angry or nasty because they are simply doing their job. I tell them that I am his mother and request that they tell my son that I've called and implore him to sign the release so I can speak to the doctors and nurses who are caring for him. I also politely request that they tell my son I love him. It is of upmost importance to show that you genuinely care for your loved one. It's also extremely important to make it obvious that you are going to be diligent in your efforts to check on their care.

When someone is transported to a psychiatric facility in four-point restraints and chemically restrained, he or she is not able to sign releases or advocate for themselves. You become their sole advocate. My sons have urinated on themselves while chemically and physically restrained because they were so sedated they were unable to voice that they needed to be taken out of restraints to use a bathroom. Once, while restrained, TJ bit a nurse on the finger because she wouldn't take him out of restraints to use the bathroom. The local police were called into the ER and TJ was charged with assault. He fought that charge in court for almost two years following the event. The charges were eventually dropped.

On another occasion in a hospital ER, TJ was held for more than 48 hours on a stretcher in four-point restraints while waiting for a bed in a psychiatric unit. We were unable to get any information about him due to privacy laws. TJ still has scars on his ankles from trying to struggle free of those restraints. We were later informed that, according to the state of Massachusetts law, restraints should be taken off an adult every four hours. My point is this: You are their voice and their advocate and you need to be vigilant in your efforts to get information about their care.

Kayvon is unique from TJ since he typically admits himself for psychiatric treatment. He willingly and voluntarily seeks help. He has actually called 911 himself and asked to be taken from our home to be treated due to a psychiatric emergency. He typically requests to be transported to Mclean Hospital and has always been admitted for treatment. Yet, once he's admitted, he is very reluctant to sign the release that grants me the right to seek information regarding his care. Often, it takes days or weeks until I'm able to find out how he's doing. Once, I actually called the patient phone lines located in his unit and asked a fellow patient to tell Kayvon he had a phone call. When Kayvon answered the patient phone, I demanded that he sign a release and threatened that I wouldn't visit him unless he did. It worked.

Once I find out that my son has signed a release, I ask for the names of the psychiatrist, social worker, and nurses assigned to his care. I make calls to each of them on a regular basis and check on my son's care. I visit my son as often as I am able to so that the staff working on his unit see that I am truly invested in his care. I request a family meeting that includes myself, my son, his social worker, and his psychiatrist when discharge is imminent. I'm sure they often consider me to be a pain in the neck. I don't care.

There is another method you can use in order to bypass the HIPAA laws in the State of Massachusetts. A Power of Attorney grants you permission to gain information, make health care decisions, and manage legal and financial affairs on your loved one's behalf. Signing this document allows your loved one to appoint a person or an organization to manage their affairs if they are unable to do so. Three years ago, after TJ's most recent hospitalization, I had a lawyer execute this document for both my sons. TJ granted me this right by signing me as his Power of Attorney. So far, Kayvon has refused to sign it.

CHAPTER TWENTY
Mapping the Journey

Caring for someone who is chronically ill is perpetual. The journey is endless. Their dependency on your support may become more manageable with time, waxing and waning over the years, but eventually you'll come to realize that they may be dependent on you for the rest of your life. So how can you prepare for them when the inevitable occurs? Once you are gone, who will be there to pick up the pieces and offer the financial and emotional support they may someday need? Fortunately, there are services offered to people who are considered psychiatrically disabled. The challenge is to find these services and advocate for assistance.

Obtaining assistance from institutions and government agencies that support individuals who are mentally ill is a daunting process, but extremely worthwhile. Getting help requires persistence and fortitude. You also must be aware of the requirements entailed by your state agencies. For instance, in Massachusetts, my sons were deemed to be eligible for services from the Department of Mental Health because they were both hospitalized, diagnosed with mental illness, and received care in a psychiatric facility two or more times during a 12-month period. Had either of them been hospitalized only one time in 12 months, they may not have been eligible for services from the Department of Mental Health (DMH).

The Department of Mental Health offers a plethora of services to qualified individuals. The services that are offered by DMH provide clinical, rehabilitative, and residential options for children, adolescents, and adults who have been diagnosed with serious mental illness. My sons have been assigned case workers who visit them on a regular basis and assist them in gaining a wide array of community based mental health services. The services my sons have received have included residential options, case management, in-home treatment from a visiting nurse, dual diagnosis treatment, day programs, and support for employment. In my opinion, this agency is understaffed and minimally funded, but the services that are available offer tremendous support. The case workers have far too many clients assigned to them and work countless hours for minimal pay. They are angels.

As soon as Kayvon and TJ are discharged from a psychiatric facility, they are urged to attend a partial day program ran by a community outreach program for outpatient care. Typically, they attend this type of program for at least two weeks. While attending the program, they receive counseling for mental health, addiction, and medication, coupled with symptom management. During the day, while attending the partial program, they also attend group therapy sessions themed on recovery and wellness. These programs are funded by private insurance or, as in my son's case, government-funded health insurance. Leaving a psychiatric facility after a typical hospitalization of two to eight weeks without this type of "step-down" program may prove to be devastating. The support and watchful eye that these partial programs offer closely follow a psychiatric hospitalization and are extremely valuable.

Once the partial program has ended, it's vital that the DMH case worker maintains regular contact with his or her client.

However, the dilemma that I have encountered happens if the ball is eventually dropped. DMH case workers are overworked, underpaid, and assigned far too many clients. It has been my experience that the case workers will begin by servicing their client on a weekly basis but will drop down to bi-weekly or monthly visits once they feel that the client is "out of the woods" and mentally stable. If a client moves or changes their living arrangement, and the case worker is not informed, the client eventually falls through the cracks of the mental health system. This type of miscommunication led to regrettable circumstances for Kayvon.

Kayvon moved to Boston while attending Massachusetts College of Art. His case worker, who was originally assigned to him, worked solely in the Wakefield area. For some reason, when Kayvon moved, his case was not forwarded to the DMH office in Boston. Kayvon was left to his own devices in a new apartment while attending a new college. His therapist and psychiatrist also were located in the Wakefield area, making it difficult for him to keep routine appointments. During that time, his father was battling Stage 4 cancer. I was preoccupied with my husband's daily chemotherapy and radiation treatments. I had virtually no time to keep track of how Kayvon was doing, and assumed he was still taking his mood stabilizers and routinely meeting with his therapist. It was the perfect storm. Kayvon had no support and began to slip mentally. He moved to Boston in September 2013. He was arrested six months later for placing a backpack on the Boston Marathon finish line in April 2014. I don't place blame on the Department of Mental Health for that incident. Kayvon simply fell through the cracks of a system that is overburdened and underfunded.

Since then, Kayvon has received visits from his DMH case worker on a regular basis. They've helped him to locate psychiatrists and therapists in the Boston area, making recommendations and assisting him in getting appointments. His case worker now visits his apartment bi-weekly and assesses his mental health by observing him while in his own environment. I have the phone number for the case worker assigned to him and will contact him if I feel that Kayvon's mental health is slipping and he may require more support. The point I want to make here is that the Department of Mental Health provides invaluable services to its clients. In light of the fact that there are far too many clients and far too few case workers in the system, once in a while you may need to provide a gentle nudge to ensure your family member is getting the services to which he or she is entitled.

Other services available in Massachusetts and perhaps other states, are the Emergency Service Programs. ESP services are community based and bring support to individuals in crisis. In Massachusetts, the ESPs are called in to evaluate and assess whether an individual requires hospitalization for a psychiatric emergency. The purpose of the ESP is to respond rapidly, assess effectively, and deliver a course of treatment to ensure safety and stabilize the crisis in a manner that allows an individual to receive medically necessary services. The ESP works in conjunction with the DMH. It is important to learn the contact information for the closest ESP affiliated with the DMH in your family member's area. It may be another avenue to turn to for assistance during a psychiatric emergency, especially during times when your family member doesn't reside with you.

We once had to turn to the ESP located in Boston for assistance with TJ. This program is called the Boston Emergency Service Team or B.E.S.T. TJ had recently moved to an apartment he found on Craigslist. He was 19 years old and felt compelled to live on his own. Unfortunately, he insisted on making this move far too soon following a recent psychiatric hospitalization. We knew he was not yet fully stable and were aware that he was still slightly hypomanic. Nonetheless, he was a force to be reckoned with. He didn't want to live with us. He thought it would be a good idea to live on his own, and insisted that living with roommates in Brighton, Massachusetts, and finding a job would provide the change he needed to pull his life together. He thought it would be a fresh start. He just wanted to do what other "normal" 19-year-olds were doing. As a parent of a child with a chronic illness, I realize how enticing it is to want your child to enjoy the life experiences that similarly aged children experience. We were concerned about the move, but we truly hoped it would work out. Unfortunately, it didn't.

From the moment we began moving TJ into his apartment, I could see his tension and anxiety escalate. He grew more and more agitated and kept leaving the apartment to smoke and pace the sidewalk. While moving in his belongings, we met TJ's roommate and exchanged phone numbers. I told him to call me in case of an emergency. I suppose at the time, his roommate was unaware of the true reason I wanted to give him my phone number. He probably gathered that I wanted to exchange contact information in case TJ got into an accident or didn't pay his rent on time. Typical worries for a parent of a typical 19-year-old. TJ insisted that we didn't reveal his psychiatric disability to his roommate. We honored his wishes.

Those first few nights away from home were far from pleasant for TJ. His mental health de-escalated rapidly. Several times in the middle of the night, TJ would call us sobbing helplessly pleading with us to come and take him home. He was frantic because he couldn't sleep. He told us he felt like killing himself. Just when we would be nearly out the door ready to drive into Boston and rescue him, he'd call back to convince us he was OK and just needed more time to adjust. It didn't take long for TJ's roommate to discover there was a problem. Within a week, he called and pleaded with me to take TJ out of the apartment. He told us that TJ was having some sort of mental breakdown. He said that TJ's room was littered with empty bottles of alcohol and that drugs were strewn all over the floor. TJ was playing deafening music all day and night. He actually informed us that he had a family member who was bipolar and suspected that TJ may be as well. I apologized for his trouble and promised I would help. I contacted the BEST program and organized a stakeout.

TJ's roommate requested that we have TJ removed from the apartment while he was not there. He feared that TJ would quickly realize that he ratted him out and expressed apprehension of potential retaliation. He only knew TJ for one week yet was afraid of what TJ might be capable of doing if the police showed up while he was present. We devised a plan. I called BEST and explained the situation. I also provided them with the name of TJ's DMH case worker and told them of his most recent hospitalization. I also mentioned that TJ had called us once in the middle of the night threatening to kill himself. That one statement provided all the ammunition needed to set the wheels in motion.

BEST told us they would notify DMH and the local police. They let us know of an approximate time of arrival at TJ's apartment and requested we be nearby to positively identify him. We drove into Boston and parked our car a block away from TJ's apartment. We didn't want TJ to see our car or spot us, so we waited in our car for the police to arrive. I remember feeling that the entire scene was surreal. Here we were, sitting in our car essentially watching and waiting for the police to come and take our 19-year-old son away. I also remember the feeling of anguish I felt when the police car finally pulled up in front of TJ's apartment. All sorts of agonizing second thoughts began to gnaw at me. Were we doing the right thing? Should we have waited a little longer for him to adjust to his new living arrangement? Will he hate us when he discovers what we did?

The entire ordeal didn't take long to complete once the police arrived. TJ had actually stepped out of his apartment mere seconds prior to the police cruiser pulling up. The police discovered him smashing his guitar on the sidewalk in front of his apartment. Two police officers got out of the cruiser, carefully approached TJ and asked him his name. TJ gave them a fake name and bolted. The two officers began chasing TJ around the block while requesting back-up. Within a minute, several other police cruisers came screeching to the scene along with ambulances and a fire truck. TJ was caught, placed in an ambulance, and brought to Massachusetts General Hospital to be evaluated. The stakeout was successful. TJ's dream of living on his own was not. At age 19, he was clearly not ready to live independently. He's now 32 and living on his own quite successfully. As difficult as it was at the time, we now realize we did the right thing. And TJ doesn't hate me for calling BEST that day and getting him the help he needed.

Social Security offers disability income for individuals who have chronic physical and psychological disabilities. The federal government has set very stringent parameters and guidelines in order for an individual to qualify for a psychiatric disability status in order to receive Social Security Disability Income. The individual must be able to prove that he or she is permanently disabled or suffering from a condition that has lasted or is expected to last for more than 12 calendar months. There are two federal programs which provide assistance to disabled individuals. Social Security Disability Insurance (SSDI) is funded by the Social Security tax fund, so individuals who qualify as disabled under the above criteria also must have sufficient tax credits in order to qualify for payments. The work-credit requirement can be somewhat less for applicants under the age of 22 as was the case with TJ. He had earned work credits while working in high school and was considered eligible for SSDI because of his psychiatric disability status beginning at age 18. Supplemental Security Income (SSI) is need based, there are no work requirements and the program is financed through general tax revenues. In order to qualify for SSI, individuals must be over 65 years old or legally blind or disabled and have total assets of less than $3,000. Kayvon has qualified for SSI because he had not gained sufficient work credits but was considered disabled at age 18.

It is of extreme importance to keep records of all hospitalizations and documentation of psychiatric appointments. When applying for SSDI or SSI, the primary reason for denial is the inability of a claimant to prove the severity of the illness due to insufficient medical records or other documentation. The process for applying for SSDI or SSI can be daunting. While TJ and Kayvon were hospitalized at McLean Hospital, their social workers helped to facilitate the process. I was not even aware that this type of monetary assistance existed for my sons. At the time, we were informed that each son qualified for assistance because their psychiatric disability was chronic and severe, they were each diagnosed before the age of 19, and were each hospitalized at least two times in a 12-month period.

If you asked me if I were pleased that my sons qualified for public assistance, my answer would be no. Of course, I'd rather that they were capable of seeking gainful employment. The amount of monthly income they receive from SSDI and SSI is minimal, barely enough to survive and considered below poverty level. Because of that, they also rely on me to garnish their day-to-day living expenses. I'm fairly certain they may be reliant on me for the rest of my life. However, I won't be around forever, and it gives me peace of mind to know that once I'm gone, they will be taken care of.

Monthly payments of SSDI and SSI are paid in a lump sum by the third day of the month. The tricky part of this, particularly in the case of someone who may be manic, is budgeting the monthly payment sensibly. Receiving a lump payment of money, regardless of the amount, has always been far too enticing for both of my sons to manage in a responsible manner. Typical household bills such as rent, utility payments, and food have often taken a backseat to more extravagant needless items often purchased on a whim while manic or grandiose. Far too often, I've received calls from my sons telling me they are not able to pay rent or other household bills because they ran out of money well before the end of the month. For this reason, the government has set up a system called the Social Security Representative Payee.

The reason the government has set up this program is because many people who collect disability payments are mentally ill, addicted to drugs or alcohol, or have come to a point in their lives in which they are no longer able to handle their finances. The job of the representative payee is to manage the immediate needs of the disabled individual. The payee needs to keep accurate records of all financial transactions and always act in the best interest of the disability recipient when distributing the funds. The representative payee can be an individual or an organization. Typically, a relative or close friend serves as the payee. An organization such as a local Community Based Flexible Support (CBFS) program operated by the Department of Mental Health also can appoint a representative payee who will collect a nominal monthly fee for this service. I have acted as a representative payee for both of my sons.

Once, while TJ was manic and paranoid, he accused me of stealing his SSDI. He "fired" me and appointed a new representative payee who worked at his local CBFS. When TJ recovered from this particular episode of mania, it didn't take him long to realize his mistake. Having me act as his representative payee was far more convenient than relying on an organization that only operated on a typical work week schedule. With me as his representative payee, TJ was able to contact me to request money at all hours. That was not the case when working with an organization designated payee.

There are other resources available to disabled individuals, which help them manage while living on a limited budget. The U.S. government provides a monthly supplement for purchasing nutritious food called the Supplemental Nutrition Assistance Program or SNAP. This program often was once referred to as "food stamps" but is now a debit card set with a monthly amount that is used for groceries. Generally, disabled individuals will qualify for SNAP since they receive SSDI or SSI. The monthly disbursement placed on the SNAP card is determined by monthly income and family size. The advantage of having a SNAP card is that it allows disabled individuals to have supplemental income for food. The disadvantages are that it allows for the purchase of food items only and not prepared food. If a disabled person is not able to conveniently prepare food, they may be at a disadvantage. The SNAP card cannot be used for items such as toilet paper, paper towels, trash bags, personal hygiene products, cleaning supplies, or other typical household items purchased in a grocery store or market. Therefore, a person on a limited budget has to rely on his or her complementary cash flow to purchase these items. Or, like TJ and Kayvon often do, raid my kitchen and bathroom cabinets when they come to visit. The Massachusetts Rehabilitation Commission (MRC) has been a precious service to TJ and Kayvon. It is a state governed and publicly funded organization that offers vocational assistance to persons who are disabled. MRC offers comprehensive career counseling, planning, and job search assistance. MRC also has programs such as Ticket to Work that allows individuals with disabilities the option of working without compromising disability benefits. MRC also offers in-state tuition assistance for qualified individuals who wish to attend college. Both TJ and Kayvon took advantage of this benefit, each of them attending and graduating from a Massachusetts state university.

The Department of Mental Health has been an invaluable resource for connecting TJ and Kayvon to multiple services that may be available to them that we were totally unaware of. A prime example is the Transportation Access Pass or TAP pass. The TAP pass offers reduced fares on public transportation such as commuter trains, buses, and subways to persons with disabilities. They also qualify for fuel assistance based on both their status as disabled and low income.

Health insurance is perhaps the most significant benefit that a disabled person is dependent on. Medical costs are often stunning for treating any chronic illness, including mental illness. The cost of hospitalization for treating a psychiatric emergency is exorbitant because the time it may take to stabilize a psychotic, manic, or severely depressed patient can often last over six weeks. Once released from 24-hour care, the patient often requires post-hospitalization care in a partial or day program for an additional length of time. Coupled with those immediate and urgent expenses are the day-to-day medical and therapeutic expenses required to manage mental illness such as medication, psychiatry visits, and cognitive therapy. Fortunately, there are federal health insurance options, such as Medicare, that will automatically insure a disabled individual who is eligible to receive SSDI or SSI. The state of Massachusetts also offers MassHealth to individuals who don't have significant means to obtain and pay for private health insurance. Living in a state such as Massachusetts proves to be advantageous for individuals who live with chronic illnesses and don't have the means to pay for treatment.

It has taken many years, countless applications and phone calls, and relentless reminders to my sons to take the time to seek out and take advantage of the services to which they are entitled. But it has been accomplished. I can rest assured that once I'm no longer there to pick up the pieces or be there for financial and emotional support, they are going to be OK. I have navigated and mapped the course. And, if they continue to follow this map on their own, they will survive.

CHAPTER TWENTY-ONE

Rider in the Storm

I suppose by now you're wondering how I've survived the past 15 years without going crazy myself. I wish I had a dollar for the amount of times people have asked me that. I've been told by friends and family members that I am the strongest person they know. But, I truly am not that strong. I can think of at least 100 situations that are far worse than raising two sons who are mentally ill. Fortunately, I have developed coping mechanisms that have helped me deal with the arduous and wearisome task of managing my sons' illnesses and the often bizarre and exasperating symptoms that characterize their illness. I have learned many coping strategies over the past 15 years. However, I consider the one mechanism that defines me, the one thing that I refuse to be and the most likely the most important thing that has helped me, is that I refuse to be a victim.

I am not a victim of my sons' illnesses. I refuse to allow their illnesses to make the quality of my life suffer. I don't dwell on the circumstances or the outcomes caused by their mental illness while they are symptomatic. I refuse to be a martyr to the collateral damage that is often caused as a result of their illness. I take care of myself. Over the years, I have learned that it's equally important to maintain my mental, emotional, and physical health as it is to keep check of their health. Often, since their initial diagnoses, I have felt sorrow for my sons. But, I have never felt bad for myself. I am not into self-pity and have never expected anyone to feel sorry for me. Yes, it's true that mental illness sucks. Sure, it's challenging to raise a child with mental illness. However, I'm not the one who is mentally ill. I can choose to be strong while being compassionate. Over the years I have learned that in order to survive, I have to be compassionately indifferent.

What does it mean to be compassionately indifferent? For me, it means that I don't allow my sons manic behavior to get the best of me. A therapist once warned me against "getting caught in their web." She explained that most often, a bipolar person who is experiencing mania will treat the person whom they most care for the worst. So, believe me when I tell you that I've been treated very inappropriately by both of my sons plenty of times. While manic, Kayvon badgers me for money, making monetary demands that are preposterous and nonsensical. He pleads, threatens, and makes ridiculous arguments for the many reasons he feels that I owe him money. I have learned to simply listen to his rant, but gently suggest a logical alternative such as seeking a part-time job. I have learned that arguing with him gets me nowhere. It just gets me more tangled in his web.

Kayvon has resorted to texting me to F*Off and telling me that he hates me when I refuse to give him more money. I don't ever feel compelled to hand him money when he treats me like that. I choose to ignore him and will often block his phone calls if he continues to hound me for money or continues to treat me inappropriately. TJ has told me he hates me, has jumped out of my moving car while yelling at me, belittled me, sworn at me, and physically pushed me. I have learned that fighting back with words or actions will only get us both into more trouble. As difficult as it is at the time, I learned that it's far better to turn the other cheek and remain compassionately indifferent.

I am a "glass half full" type of person. I was told by a therapist that my attitude toward life in general epitomized the saying, "When life hands you lemons, make lemonade." For example, I remember a time when both of my sons were hospitalized at the same time. I spent my Sundays traveling one hour to Bridgewater State Hospital to visit TJ, and at the end of his visit, getting back in my car to travel another hour to Belmont to visit Kayvon who was hospitalized at McLean Hospital. I remember shrugging my shoulders and thinking that at least I was traveling in the right direction since Belmont was on my way home instead of farther away. I am always able to find some shred of positivity in the worst of times. Always, after enduring weeks of manic chaos in my house, when either of my sons were safely hospitalized I could always breathe a huge sigh of relief. Instead of dwelling on the sad fact that my sons were being committed to a psychiatric facility, I felt relief that they were finally being taken care of by qualified professionals. My house was peacefully quiet and I could once again sleep soundly. I remember feeling happy that I was able to get into their bedrooms to organize the chaos and tackle their laundry. I have always felt, even under the most dire circumstances, that my situation was far more manageable than what other people had to deal with.

I also credit my perseverance on my ability to compartmentalize. This is a defense mechanism that helps me to cope, particularly when I'm in a vulnerable situation. The ability to place my sons' struggles on the back burner and forget about them while focusing entirely on my work has helped me manage during times of intense stress. I have taught group exercise for more than 30 years. When I am teaching group exercise in front of a large group of students who rely on my timely cues and motivation, I am able to lose myself in the moment. I am entirely focused on the task at hand. I am "in the zone."

That one hour of leading a group of sweat-soaked, happy people while listening to loud, upbeat music is captivating. I am doing something that I am passionate about. I am an energetic, inspiring, joy-filled leader. I am totally in charge. For that hour, in front of all those people who chose to work out with me, I am simply a group exercise instructor. Not once, not even for a brief moment, do I think about my sons. Choosing this vocation has helped me maintain my identity while relieving a great deal of stress. Whether it has been the release of endorphins through exercise or the sheer fact that I don't have a minute to allow my mind to wander from the task at hand, teaching group exercise has been an enormous stress reliever.

Another strategy that has worked for me is to take control when I lose control. As a parent, spouse, family member of someone with mental illness, one of the most frustrating and challenging aspects of the disease is that ultimately, you have no control over their illness. I think this may be particularly difficult for a parent since the role of a parent is to nurture. During the past 15 years, there have been countless times when I was aware that my sons weren't taking their medications, had missed therapy sessions, were abusing alcohol or drugs, not sleeping, or not following up with medication management. Initially, I try to make gentle reminders in order to carefully coax them into taking better care of themselves. It doesn't help. As their moods grow progressively less stable resulting in mania and psychosis, I begin to feel like a rider in the storm. I can only sit back and helplessly watch the storm brewing, its intensity magnifying to the point of no return. There is no turning back. My only option is to wait until the storm passes.

Once they are finally hospitalized for treatment, I am able to gain some sense of mastery over the situation. I am no longer a bystander who is helplessly trapped in the eye of the storm. I am able to regain control and advocate for their care. I make phone calls to their in-patient treatment teams, notify the Department of Mental Health and speak to their caseworker, get in touch with their therapist and psychiatrist, and inform their friends of the current situation. Taking action and regaining some power, even it seems like a mere shred of control, helps me feel less like a helpless passenger who is riding out the storm and more like a force to be reckoned with sitting in the driver's seat.

Talking to people helps to keep me sane. I have been extremely fortunate to have a group of caring and empathetic friends who are always available to listen. They have never judged me or my sons. They aren't there to offer advice or to try to fix things, they are simply there for me. They support me even if they don't necessarily agree with me. Their primary concern is my health and well-being and they will do whatever it takes to help me manage the stress that often comes while caring for my sons. If they call me to check in and sense that things aren't going well, they will offer to take me out to chat and commiserate over a cup of coffee or a glass of wine. I know they love me no matter what I've had to deal with, but I also realize that they care about and are truly compassionate for my sons.

For two days, following the incident when Kayvon placed the backpack on the Boston Marathon finish line, my entire neighborhood was under siege by the press. I had to draw the shades, unplug my home phone, and hide in my house. My friends came to rescue me. They boldly crossed in front of the cameras, avoiding microphones that were shoved in front of them, to keep me company. They brought food, flowers, and wine, most importantly they brought comfort in the eye of the storm and strong shoulders to lean on. I remember telling them that all I wanted to do was to take my dog out for a short walk. Three of us left the house with the dog while wearing heavy hooded jackets to disguise ourselves. We were only able to walk a block away from the house when a reporter discovered us, figured out that I had left the house, and began running in our direction along with her camera crew. Before I knew it, another friend pulled up beside me in her van, let me into the backseat, and sped off. I have true friends whom I can count on no matter what.

Talking to a professional is essential. A therapist can help you cope with the stress and conflicting feelings of living with or raising someone with mental illness. In times of dire stress, when I've felt like the weight of the world was resting on my shoulders and I had nowhere else to turn, my therapist has been my savior. Speaking with a therapist is safe, you can rely on them to be confidential while remaining nonjudgmental. My therapist has offered many strategies for changing the self-destructive behaviors that I was unaware of when dealing with my sons' mental illnesses. With my therapist's help, I have learned how to be better at handling the manipulative aspect of their bipolar disorder. I also have learned how harmful it is to be an enabler. I've learned the difference between helping my sons and enabling them. I've learned that enabling or trying to solve their problem will only exacerbate the problem. Sometimes, it's better to let them fall flat on their face. Then and only then, will their dysfunctional behavior begin to change.

Misery enjoys company. It's nice to know that you're not all alone in the world when dealing with struggles. Sometimes, when I've felt like banging my head against a wall, attending a support group has helped. There's nothing like sitting with a group of people who have similar stories, difficulties, and challenges. However, I'm warning you that it can be depressing, too! Sitting in a group meeting while listening to tales of woe has left me feeling defeated instead of supported at times. I remember feeling like I wanted to run as fast as I could out of one group meeting while one parent after another shared horrific stories of their mentally ill children. That was not at all helpful. I came to that meeting for support not sadness.

You need to find a support group meeting that suits you. A support group that offers helpful advice, a sense of community, and emotional support led by a trained facilitator has been the type of group that has helped me the most. There are many support groups available to parents, spouses, and family members. I highly recommend attending a meeting offered by NAMI, the National Alliance on Mental Illness. NAMI is the nation's largest organization dedicated to education, advocacy, and awareness of mental illness. This organization offers support group meetings led by trained facilitators throughout the United States.

Our family dog Lucy afforded perhaps the most significant means of stress relief and comfort to our entire family during the past 15 years. She was a gem of a dog, an adorable Schnoodle with a calm and soothing demeanor. Her disposition proved to be ideal for living in a household fraught with constant turmoil. She rarely barked and was never frightened by loud noises or mayhem. She loved to cuddle and befriended everyone she met. At the age of 2, Lucy was trained to be a pet therapy dog for Caring Canines Visiting Therapy Dogs Inc. For the following 12 years, she made more than 150 visits to nursing homes, hospitals, hospice centers, and even provided relief to victims of the Boston Marathon bombing.

Lucy also was our family's private therapy dog. We all adored her. There were countless times, prominently when either TJ or Kayvon were manic, that Lucy became the sole instrument that we could all rely on for comfort. When we were too angry or frightened to speak directly to each other, we could speak through Lucy. I recall a time when TJ was manic and high on drugs. He called me up to his bedroom because he wanted to show me something "cool." When I entered his room, he proceeded to throw Lucy in the air, over his bed, convinced that she could fly. I remember how frightening it was to watch him throw her across his bed, yet thankful that Lucy wasn't freaking out herself. Instead of screaming at him, I seized the opportunity to use my "Lucy voice" to convince him to stop. I pleaded in my most convincing Lucy voice, "Please don't throw me TJ. It makes me nervous because I really can't fly and I may get hurt." He stopped. He started to cry and apologized to Lucy for frightening her. Had I simply yelled frantically at him, he probably would've injured her unintentionally.

Our mutual love for Lucy was the one common thread that often tied our family together. During times when TJ or Kayvon weren't speaking with each other, which unfortunately was more often than not, they could speak through Lucy. When TJ or Kayvon were first hospitalized and angry at me and refused communication, I sent them cards from Lucy. My "Lucy cards" gave me the opportunity to express my concern and love to them in a nonthreatening manner. Lucy was often allowed to visit Kayvon while he was hospitalized at McLean Hospital. Fellow patients were given the opportunity to pet Lucy during her visit on the unit. It was truly amazing to witness how much calmer these patients grew as they petted Lucy.

Dogs provide comfort in the storm. Their love is unconditional. Walking Lucy, patting Lucy, and cuddling with Lucy provided immense stress relief to our family. She was a special dog. Her temperament was ideal for a family struggling to find peace and a sense of normalcy. We will always be thankful for and truly value the 14½ years she lived with us. Lucy was a gift.

Finally, there have certainly been times when all my true and tried coping strategies have failed. I remember a day that stands out in my memory as a situation that foremost exemplifies stress at its worse. I was at Dana-Farber Cancer Institute, sitting in a chemotherapy treatment room with my husband during the time when he was battling the final stages of cancer. I was frazzled, emotionally and physically exhausted from the months of dealing with my husband's treatments. I was beginning to lose hope that he would survive his illness. While sitting in his room watching the nurses administer chemotherapy, I received a frantic phone call from Kayvon. He wanted to admit himself to McLean Hospital. He sounded manic and told me he was paranoid and needed help. He asked that I pick him up at his Boston apartment and drive him to McLean Hospital in Belmont, only five miles away. I left my daughter with my husband and told them I would return as soon as I could. I drove Kayvon to McLean Hospital and assisted with his admittance.

As soon as he was safely admitted for psychiatric treatment, I got in my car and drove back to Dana-Farber Cancer Institute in Boston to rejoin my husband and daughter. I entered the hospital and began to navigate my way back to my husband and daughter. I got lost. I began to sweat, my heart began to race, I experienced tunnel vision, and panicked. I was experiencing a full-blown panic attack. I called my daughter and told her I was lost. She could tell by the tone of my voice that I was not OK. She asked me to explain to her exactly where I was and told me to wait for her. She found me crying, curled up in a fetal position in the middle of a couch located in front of the Jimmy Fund clinic. She knew at that time, that I reached my limit. I could not tolerate any more stress on my own. I was at the end of my rope. I was having difficulty sleeping and was not eating regular meals. She suggested that I call my primary care physician and obtain an anti-anxiety medication such as Ativan.

I'm not the strongest person in the world. I am not ashamed to admit that there are times when life just gets too difficult to manage without medication. There are times when I lie awake in bed and worry. If I hear my phone ping to announce a text message in the middle of the night or very early hours of the morning, I worry that it's one of my sons in trouble. I don't rely on an anti-anxiety medication to get me through every night. There are months that go by when I don't need to take an anti-anxiety medication at all. However, for those evenings when I can't sleep, when the weight of the world is resting on my shoulders, when I feel victimized by the demons of my sons' illnesses and the worries for their future, it's nice to have something available to help me sleep. I am simply taking care of myself and doing what I must to stay well.

CHAPTER TWENTY-TWO

A Family Derailed

Mental illness has affected my family on many levels. Our family dynamics were forever changed on the day that TJ was diagnosed with bipolar disorder. But, not all change is bad. In many ways, having a family member (or two) with mental illness has helped us better manage other challenges that life has thrown at us. It has made us more resilient, more tolerant, and more able to roll with the punches. Each of my family members has been affected by mental illness in their own unique manner. The sheer presence of mental illness in our family has etched a future that is not what we originally envisioned. We were sidetracked by mental illness and are now forging our own journey. Our family chemistry has changed, and we are continually trying to stay on track and exist as a family.

If you asked me to describe the feeling I have about how mental illness has affected my family, I would describe the feeling as grief. In my heart, there exists a profound sense of loss. I often mourn for what could have been. My sons are alive, yet I feel sorrow that they have lost that sense of normalcy that other men have at their age.

They struggle daily with the side effects of medication and the stigma associated with being mentally ill. The typical adult milestones such as dating, getting married, having children, and achieving a career have each been curtailed by the daily management of their illness. I'm not speculating that all these things are no longer attainable. I'm just stating that mental illness makes all of these things more difficult to attain. Face it or not, it's difficult to deny that the stigma exists. If TJ or Kayvon enter into a long-term relationship, that person must be fully prepared and aware of the implications of their illness. My hope is that they are able to someday find the right person and establish a loving relationship. That person may just be more difficult to find.

During the past 15 years, I also have learned the importance of being able to change my perspective of what constitutes success and happiness. I was going to state here that I have learned to lower my standards, but that is not entirely the case. I still hold hope that my sons will find success and happiness in their lives. Still, the milestones that are customarily used to measure success have changed. Dwelling on the typical milestones that my friends and relatives celebrate and post on social media can, and often do, make me feel resentful. Will I ever live to hold a grandchild, dance with my son at his wedding, or have bragging rights to their successful career? When the green monster of jealousy rears her ugly head, I try not to dwell on what could have been nor what may never be. Instead, I try to focus on all the notable milestones they have been able to accomplish while battling mental illness.

One of the proudest moments for me as a mother occurred while attending an Alcoholics Anonymous meeting. I was invited to attend the meeting to witness TJ be awarded his five-year sobriety token. I had never been to an AA meeting, and had no idea what to expect. I sat at the meeting attended by more than 100 people and observed while each one filed in and took their seat. The group consisted of professional people arriving from work in suits and ties, young tattooed adults in their early 20s, middle-aged women and men, and older adults who appeared disheveled and worn down, men and women from all walks of life. The one common thread that they all willingly acknowledged, was that they were alcoholics.

TJ was asked to speak during the meeting. He confidently walked to the podium to begin his speech. He introduced himself in the same manner as all who attend AA, "Hi, I'm TJ and I'm an alcoholic." He spoke of his struggle with substance abuse and mental illness. He brazenly documented some of the most profoundly disturbing events in his life with grace and confidence. TJ's story and the attainment of his five-year sobriety token was applauded and celebrated by all who attended that meeting. This incident serves as an example of how my perspective has changed. That evening, listening to my 25-year-old son document how he pulled himself up by his bootstraps to battle addiction was perhaps one of the proudest and happiest moments of my life.

I am proud to note that TJ has recently completed his 10th year of sobriety. He diligently attends AA meetings and speaks at commitment meetings in hospitals, substance abuse clinics, and correctional facilities. He also is trained to act as a peer counselor for NAMI. He attends NAMI meetings to speak about his experience of living with bipolar disorder and substance abuse. He shares stories of his struggles with bipolar disorder, how he has learned to accept his illness, ways in which he manages his illness, and his hopes and dreams for the future.

I also am thrilled that both of my sons have finally obtained their undergraduate degrees. Unlike most young adults who are able to obtain their undergraduate degree in five years or less, it took both TJ and Kayvon more than 10 years to earn their college diploma. They each had to jump over many hurdles in order to complete this accomplishment, being hospitalized several times, changing schools, and moving. They never gave up. The determination and fortitude it took them to get to this point in their life is a testament to their strength of character. For me, it's priceless.

Our family has had to learn about acceptance. We have learned to accept the various ways in which mental illness has changed our family dynamics. Sometimes, we have to accept the fact that we need to make sacrifices in order to keep peace. I have to make accommodations when planning holidays and family events since TJ and Kayvon have difficulty tolerating each other. Kayvon's personality disorder and its ensuing characteristics have driven a wedge between himself and TJ. He has said things about TJ that TJ considers to be unforgivable. To put it bluntly, they can't even stand being in the same room with each other. Planning a holiday such as Christmas can be extremely challenging. I have to carefully and tactfully accommodate my sons by planning the holiday in shifts so that I am able to celebrate the holiday with them both while keeping them separate. It stinks for me and for their sister. We reluctantly accept yet hope that perhaps this will someday change.

One of the most dispiriting consequences that I've had to accept is the fact that my daughter, JoEllen, has chosen to forgo motherhood. She is afraid. She dreads that she may possibly give birth to a child that will inherit bipolar disorder. She doesn't want to risk the chance of potentially having to raise a child with mental illness. In the words she has stated to me, "I don't want to have to go through what you have had to endure while raising the boys." I consider this to be one of the most unfortunate ways in which mental illness has affected our family. Could JoEllen adopt children? Of course, she could. Yet, I have had to honor her choice and learn to accept that I may never live to hold a biological grandchild of my own. So, I have granddogs and grandchickens. I love and accept each and every one of my furry and feathery grandchildren.

JoEllen also has revealed her worry that she may someday be diagnosed with bipolar disorder herself. Women are typically diagnosed with a mood disorder in their middle to late 30's. I can certainly empathize with her anxiety. She is now 35 and thankfully has not exhibited any of the signs that characterize a mood disorder. Nevertheless, she admits that with every passing year, she breathes a huge sigh of relief that her moods are still stable.

During the final stages of my husband's life, while he was receiving hospice at home and resolutely accepting the fact he had lost his one-year battle with cancer, he told me what he wanted for me once he was gone. He made me promise that I would try to find someone else to share my life with. He wasn't concerned about his sons' well-being. He knew that I was capable of taking care of TJ and Kayvon. He wanted me to find someone who would take care of me.

At that time, I couldn't possibly imagine that I would be able to find someone who was as patient or strong of a companion. Tommy was my partner and together we were a great team. When the boys grew assaultive due to mania or psychosis, Tommy was the one who physically battled with them in order to get them help. He was the one who chased TJ or Kayvon around the neighborhood when they fled as the police arrived at our house to take them to the hospital. Countless times, he bravely dodged their aggression when they fought him with knives, golf clubs, and fists. When it came to dealing with the mania and psychosis caused by our sons' mental illnesses, we both rose to the occasion and worked together like a well-oiled machine. Tommy did the dirty work. I dealt with the aftermath. I was the one who picked up the pieces after the storm. I made the calls to the hospitals and countless psychiatrists, social workers and therapists, or plead with the mental health system and the legal system to get them the help they needed. I knew I would miss Tommy and how well we worked together to help our sons. I wondered how I could possibly manage all of this alone. I couldn't imagine finding someone who would take care of me and accept all the baggage that would accompany me in a new relationship.

A year and a half after Tommy died, I began to get lonely. Dating, after being with one man for 45 years, was an intimidating undertaking to say the least. I bravely took on the somewhat painstaking conquest of online dating and began my search. When I met Jim, I was instantly attracted to his honesty, intelligence, and kind demeanor. By our second date, we both sensed that this could possibly develop into a long-term relationship. That night, after we enjoyed a nice dinner together, I told him that I needed to tell him something important concerning my family. I felt that this was something that needed to be revealed before we continued to date each other. I felt compelled to tell Jim about TJ and Kayvon. Jim listened attentively as I recounted the story of how Kayvon placed the backpack on the Boston Marathon finish line on the one-year anniversary of the tragic bombing. He sat quietly while I told him about TJ's experiences at Bridgewater State Hospital. I explained to him that I needed to tell him these things because it was important for him to know this about me if this ever turned out to be a long-term relationship. I was the mother of two sons with mental illness. I would always be the mother of two sons with mental illness. If he felt that he wanted to continue dating me, he needed to be aware of what he was getting into. He took a deep breath, let it out, and said, "It's a lot."

It has been three years since that second date. Jim admits that he fell in love with me that night because of my strength and bravery. He is still with me and embraces my children like his own. He has attended TJ and Kayvon's college graduations. He has celebrated their birthdays and shared holidays with them. He treats my sons with patience, dignity, and respect. He also praises their talents and appreciates their unique personalities.

Jim also has been there when I've needed him during the "not so good" times. He accompanied me on many visits to McLean Hospital while Kayvon was hospitalized during the Easter holiday. He has helped to move Kayvon in and out of three apartments during the course of only two years. He tries to cheer me up when I'm overwhelmed or angry over the frustrating aspects of Kayvon's mood and personality disorder. He provides me the space and time I require to deal with the negative features of Kayvon's illness. He offers helpful suggestions while at the same time, respecting my position as Kayvon's mother. Jim has proven to be exactly the person that Tommy hoped I would find, someone who would love and take care of me.

My family is not typical. We make sacrifices to keep the peace. We have learned to accept and modulate what constitutes success and happiness. We celebrate our uniqueness and are thankful for the precious times of peace and unity. Together, our family will try to stay on the right track.

CHAPTER TWENTY-THREE

Disembarking for Now

My father has bipolar disorder. His mood disorder was referred to as "manic/depressive." I was a child growing up in a household often fraught with worry and confusion. I recall many childhood days when my parents would fight so passionately that my father would eventually storm out of the house in anger, not returning until later the next day. My siblings and I took refuge in our bedrooms and huddled together while we heard loud screaming, furniture being thrown, and doors slamming. My father was once found guilty of tax evasion and had to spend time incarcerated in jail when I was a teenager. My mother now tells us of how he shamelessly cheated on her and often spent money frivolously. He was often grandiose and exhibited many of the classic symptoms of bipolar disorder. My parents are now divorced and I'm sad to note that I rarely have any contact with my father.

Bipolar disorder may be inherited. Although this hasn't yet been proven scientifically, recent studies have shown that individuals with bipolar disorder often have relatives with similar mood, anxiety, and psychotic disorders. Neurotransmitters, or the chemicals that pass messages between the various areas of the brain, are shown to be unbalanced in people who have mood disorders. The brain is producing either too few or too many. This chemical imbalance also may be genetic. Although bipolar disorder and its causes aren't yet well understood, researchers have recently suggested a connection between family history and bipolar disorder. Thirty-five years ago, when I was beginning to plan a family, I never once considered that I could one day pass this along to my own children. And, what would I have done if I had known?

Kayvon once asked me an astounding question that haunts me to this day. He was only 21 and just two years had passed since his initial diagnosis of bipolar disorder. At the time, he had recently been forced to drop out of college for the second time due to the symptoms of his bipolar disorder. We were in the car and I was driving. Out of the blue, he turned to me and asked, "If you had known that one day I'd be mentally ill, would you have still had me?" I was flabbergasted.

It has been more than eight years since he blindsided me with that question. During the course of those eight years, Kayvon's struggles with mental illness have heightened. He has been arrested, spent numerous times in psychiatric facilities, and grappled to find employment and places to live. His impulsive and explosive nature has resulted in ruined relationships with friends and family. I often wonder if he'll ever find peace and acceptance of his illness. I also worry that the characteristics of his illness may keep escalating instead of improving.

Kayvon may be mentally ill, but his mental illness does not define him as a person. He also is extremely intelligent and talented. His unique vision for fashion, design, and performance art may be idiosyncratic and provocative, but that is exactly what constitutes the essence of a true artist. When he's stable, he can be endearing, entertaining, and quite charming. He wishes to succeed someday and possess the ability to share his gifts with the world. He is persistent and sets high standards for himself, never giving up on his dreams despite countless setbacks and major disappointments.

There are many notable people with mood disorders who have lived or still live successful and full lives including actresses Catherine Zeta-Jones, Vivian Leigh, Carrie Fisher, and Linda Hamilton, musicians Sinead O'Connor, Demi Lovato, and Scott Stapp, the novelist Virginia Woolf, journalists Jane Pauley and Elizabeth Vargas, and artist Vincent van Gogh. The talents that these artists and writers have shared with the world is remarkable. They have all learned to live and succeed while coping with mood disorders or struggling with addiction. They are examples of capable, intelligent, and talented individuals who have enhanced our lives by sharing their gifts with us.

When you give birth to your child, you hope that they will live a healthy and happy life. It is our nature as parents to protect our children from suffering and pain. We work diligently to provide for them in order to ensure their comfort. They are raised and encouraged to become good, strong, capable adults who will be able to live independently and happily.

There are DNA tests available, which are administered during the early stages of pregnancy, that serve to detect abnormalities in the fetus. Parents who are informed of potential life-threatening physical conditions or cognitive abnormalities that may affect the quality of life of the child are given the option to abort the fetus. Some parents choose to take that option, others choose to sustain the pregnancy and hope for the best. I'm certain this is one of the most difficult and heart wrenching decisions a new parent has to face.

DNA tests, administered specifically to detect mental illness, performed early in a pregnancy do not exist. Perhaps in the future, a DNA test that detects the existence of a potential mood, anxiety, or substance abuse-related disorder will be available. However, it's also highly probable that medical science may hopefully develop medications that will treat these disorders more effectively and without the negative side effects. My fingers are crossed.

My answer to Kayvon's question that day was honest and forthright. Yes, even if I was provided with the knowledge that his DNA had revealed characteristics of a potential mood disorder, I would certainly go through with the pregnancy. There are no guarantees in life. No one enters this world armed with a money-back guarantee. Many children, who are born healthy, may someday succumb to catastrophic injury or life-threatening illness later on in their life. I have survived the unwelcome and surprising arrival of mental illness in my sons' lives. I realize, as a parent, that I may have had to face far more difficult situations. Luckily, I have been given the strength to deal with this.

It has been eight years since he asked me that startling question and my answer would still be the same. Kayvon is unique, one in a million. Sure, there are many days when he has challenged my patience, been unlikeable, outrageous, inappropriate, and extremely difficult, but he's still my son and I love him.

I am disembarking from this crazy train for now. It certainly has been a long and interesting journey. I am leaving the station armed with a multitude of knowledge and wealth of experience that I have gained during the course of this 15-year adventure. I have learned how to cope, how to advocate for assistance, and how to help my sons when they are in the midst of a mental health crisis. TJ has grown stronger, more confident, and accepting of his mood disorder and substance abuse issues since his initial diagnosis 15 years ago. It is my hope that Kayvon will continue to mature, seek assistance, and also learn to accept his illness. I realize that my journey has not ended. It never will. Nevertheless, the next time I climb aboard the Bipolar Express, I will not be riding alone or in the dark.

THE AUTHOR

Joie Edson is the mother of two sons who have been diagnosed with Bipolar Disorder, one at age 17 and the second son at age 19. She lives in Wakefield, Massachusetts, and earned both her undergraduate and master's degree in education from Salem State University. A retired Physical Education teacher, Joie currently teaches group exercise classes in the Greater Boston area. She has lived through inexplicable experiences, including a notable arrest of one of her sons at the Boston Marathon finish line, as a result of their illnesses. This is her story, but it also serves to shed light on the challenges other parents or families may face when raising children with mental illness.

Made in the USA
Middletown, DE
30 September 2018